English through Active Learning

— Read to Think and Speak —

TORIKAI Shinichiro
SUZUKI Natsuyo
INDA Sachiko

Asahi Press

《《《 音声ストリーミング配信 》》》

http://text.asahipress.com/free/english/

この教科書の音声は、
上記ウェブサイトにて無料で配信しています。

English through Active Learning: Read to Think and Speak

Copyright © 2019 by Asahi Press

All rights reserved. No Part of this book may be reproduced or transmitted in any form or by any means, electronic or mechanical, including photocopying, recording or by any information storage and retrieval system, without permission in writing from authors and the publisher.

イラスト：駿高泰子

はじめに

　アクティブ・ラーニングということばがよく使われるようになりました。新しい学習指導要領でも、アクティブ・ラーニングということばは使われはしないものの、学習者自らが主体的に学ぶというアクティブ・ラーニング本来の考え方が導入され、教えてもらう授業から自分たちが積極的に学ぶ授業へとの転換が図られています。新たな知識や技能を学ぶということは大変な知的活動ですが、これを教員が指導し、教え込むという従来の方法では本当に学んだことにはならないのではないか、学ぶということはもっと主体的な行為であり、学習者自らがなぜ学ぶのか、何を学ぶのか、どう学ぶのかを常に反芻しつつ学ぶということこそが、本来の学びではないか、そのような考え方から生まれたのがアクティブ・ラーニングです。

　本書は、立教大学全学共通カリキュラム運営センターの「英語R」クラスを担当した教員が、英語を学ぶとは何か、学生はどのようにして英語を学ぶのがよいのか、学生が英語をより効果的に学ぶためにはどのような授業にすればよいのか、などを話し合う過程で、自分たちでアクティブ・ラーニングを使った英語の教科書を作ってみようということになり、生まれたものです。大学生が持つ知的好奇心を喚起し、学生が英文を理解しようと奮闘し、題材を通して自らが考え、自分の意見を発表してゆく、その過程で結果として英語の学習が進む、そういったプロセスで英語の学習が展開してゆく授業をイメージしています。本書を使うことで、英語を学びながら学生がより知的に考え、積極的に英語を使いこなせるようになれば、幸いです。

　本書の作成にあたっては、立教大学ランゲージセンターの教育講師である長坂氏並びに松井氏から貴重なご助言を頂きました。この場をお借りして御礼を申し上げる次第です。

鳥飼慎一郎
鈴木夏代
印田佐知子

Contents

はじめに

Unit 0	この教科書の使い方	i
Unit 1	**Desert Wisdom** 砂漠が教えてくれる人生の歩み方	1
Unit 2	**The Power of Friendship** ハリウッド俳優の友情と絆	7
Unit 3	**Cell Phone Culture:** **How Cultural Differences Affect Mobile Use** ところ変わればマナーも変わる！？	13
Unit 4	**Men are from Mars, Women are from Venus** 「男女の心理」―違いを理解すればわかり合える？	19
Unit 5	**The Beginning Part of *Botchan*** 日本の小説「坊ちゃん」を英語で読むと？	25
Unit 6	***Guernica*** パブロ・ピカソが作品に込めた思いとは？	31
Unit 7	**The Art of Lying** あなたの嘘は何色？　嘘には色がある？	37
Unit 8	**Fuji-san (3,776m)** 富士山と日本人の密接な関係	43
Unit 9	**The Three Secrets to Persuasion:** **Aristotle and Ethos, Pathos, and Logos** ギリシャの哲学者に学ぶ弁論術	49
Unit 10	**Malala Yousafzai Nobel Peace Prize Lecture** ノーベル平和賞・マララさんが伝えるメッセージ	55
Unit 11	**Eating Disorders** 「摂食障害」のこころを読み解く	61
Unit 12	**Working Conditions, Death from Overwork** 「過労死」に関わる労働条件の改善策はある？	67
Unit 13	**Emotional Robots** ロボットに感情は必要か？	73
Unit 14	**Maslow's *Hierarchy of Needs*** 人間の根源的な欲求と動機づけの関係	79

Unit 0 この教科書の使い方

　本書は、題名が示すようにアクティブ・ラーニングの学習方法を使って英語を効果的に学習し、英語でコミュニケーションができるようになることを目指しています。本書にはそのための様々な工夫が施されています。

Let's Chat

　そのユニットで扱うテーマに想像を巡らすパートです。ユニットの題名から本文の内容を直感する場合もあるでしょう。おおいに想像をかき立てられることもあるでしょう。写真を見てハッと気づくこともあるでしょう。自分の英語を使って質問に答えてみましょう。自然とアクティブ・ラーニングの世界に引き込まれてゆきます。

Main Text

まずは一通りザッと読んでみましょう。知らない単語や表現があってもかまいません。この本文全体は何について述べているのか、各パラグラフの要点は何か、誰がどうした、何が起こったのか、一言でもいいので答えられるように情報を拾い集めながら読みましょう。

本文の下には丁寧な註釈が付けてあります。それを参考にして、分からない語や表現を理解しながら、もう一度読んでみましょう。霧が晴れるように本文の内容が見えてくるはずです。

Desert Wisdom

People often say that life is like climbing a mountain. Until you reach the top, there are all kinds of difficulties and troubles, and the hardest thing can be coming down from the mountain. Canadian adventurer and consultant Steve Donahue is opposed to this notion. He argues that life is really more like a desert; mountains offer a clear goal, the summit, but deserts are trackless, and people don't know for sure where to go. Donahue suggests several ways to cross the desert wisely, based on his experience.

The most important thing is to follow the compass, not the map. Do not cling to the place where you are but be aware of where you are heading. Mountains and maps have something in common — both have a clear goal and known paths and you can calculate the time to your destination. But unlike mountains, deserts usually don't have roads. Common sense is not enough and no one knows where a path may lead. Therefore, in a desert it is important to read the compass within yourself and pay heed to your own sense of direction rather than what you see. French author and pilot Antoine de Saint-Exupéry once said, "I stayed up all night reading the map. However, it was useless. I couldn't find out where I was."

(382 words)

Notes
l. 1　**Until ...**　～（する、になる）まで
l. 3　**consultant**　顧問、専門分野における相談相手
l. 4　**is opposed to ...**　～に反対する／**notion**　考え、考え方
l. 5　**a clear goal, the summit**　明確な目的地すなわち頂上（挿入句）／**trackless**　道のない
l. 8　**the compass**　羅針盤、磁石
l. 9　**cling to**　執着する、固執する／**be aware of ...**　～に気がつく
l. 11　**destination**　目的地
l. 12　**Common sense**　思慮分別、良識
l. 14　**read**　（地図や羅針盤などを）見て理解する／**pay heed to**　心にとめる、留意する／**your own sense of direction**　自分自身の方向感覚
l. 15　**Antoine de Saint-Exupéry**　アントワーヌ・ド・サン＝テグジュペリ（1900年～1944年）『星の王子様』などの作品があるフランスの作家、飛行操縦士

Graphic Organizer (G.O.)

　空所にどの単語を入れればいいのか、本文を読み返して考えてみてください。G.O. と本文との間を行きつ戻りつしながら、G.O. を完成する過程こそが、本文の内容や展開の仕方を理解する過程であり、G.O. を完成できれば、本文を日本語に訳さずに英語のママで理解したことになります。

Graphic Organizer

Life as a Desert

Adventurer Steve Donahue argues that **1.**＿＿＿＿＿ is like a desert.

⬇

Reason
Mountains offer a clear **2.**＿＿＿＿＿ , but deserts are **3.**＿＿＿＿＿ and people do not know where they are heading.

Ways to Cross the Desert (Live Life) Wisely

Tip 1
Follow the compass, not the **4.**＿＿＿＿＿ .
▶ Deserts do not have **5.**＿＿＿＿＿ , so read the compass within yourself and pay heed to your own sense of **6.**＿＿＿＿＿ .

Tip 2
7.＿＿＿＿＿ a tire when caught in sand.
▶ When you are in trouble, let some **8.**＿＿＿＿＿ out of the ego and become more **9.**＿＿＿＿＿ .

Tip 3
Rest when you come across an **10.**＿＿＿＿＿ .
▶ Restoring your **11.**＿＿＿＿＿ and looking both forward and back allows you to work more **12.**＿＿＿＿＿ .

4　English through Active Learning —Read to Think and Speak—

この教科書の使い方　iii

Active Learning

　自分で主体的に考え、意見を述べ合い、議論をし、発展的に英語学習を進めるパートです。言語に注意を向けながら、その言語を使って人の意見に耳を傾け、自分の考えを主張し、皆で協力してより面白い答えを出し合ってみてください。英語の授業がいつの間にか協働作業の場に変わってゆくことでしょう。

Active Learning

1. Listening Task

前置詞や副詞を伴う動詞（句動詞）を本文からみつけて書き出そう。次にこれらの句動詞から3つ選び、正しい短文を作って紹介しあおう。

come ＿＿＿＿＿	oppose ＿＿＿＿＿	based ＿＿＿＿＿
cling ＿＿＿＿＿	be aware ＿＿＿＿＿	pay heed ＿＿＿＿＿
stay ＿＿＿＿＿	find ＿＿＿＿＿	come ＿＿＿＿＿
speed ＿＿＿＿＿	sink ＿＿＿＿＿	get ＿＿＿＿＿

1. ＿＿＿＿＿＿＿＿＿＿＿＿＿＿＿＿＿＿＿＿＿＿＿＿＿＿＿＿＿＿＿＿＿＿＿＿＿

2. ＿＿＿＿＿＿＿＿＿＿＿＿＿＿＿＿＿＿＿＿＿＿＿＿＿＿＿＿＿＿＿＿＿＿＿＿＿

3. ＿＿＿＿＿＿＿＿＿＿＿＿＿＿＿＿＿＿＿＿＿＿＿＿＿＿＿＿＿＿＿＿＿＿＿＿＿

2. Map Task

同じ地図を手元に道順を教える人と、道順を聞いて進む人に分かれます。お互いの地図を見ないで、道順を教える人は宝の在り処を決めた場所に相手を誘導しよう。地図に山や川や小屋などの目印を自由に描き込んで教えあおう。

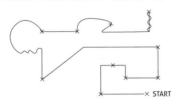

（例）Go this way for a couple of minutes until you see the big forest on your left. Then turn left and go on for about 5 minutes until you see a cottage and monument right across from each other.

Tips　道案内をするとき、このような表現が使えます。

You will see a large ---- on the right.	You will pass a -----.
It's across from the old mill.	It's on + street name
It's opposite　　It's near	It's around the corner from
Turn right at the next street	Go one more block. Then turn right.
At the next traffic lights turn ...	It's going to be on your right.

● **Expressions for This Unit**

to the North, South, East, West	Go + direction (right, left, down, up, through)	
take + road name	turn + right/left	It's on the left/right.
go straight ahead	go straight on	when you get to ...

Desert Wisdom　5

Further Thinking

　考えさせられる質問が提示されます。インターネットで調べたり、図書館に行って本を探して読んだりして、考えてみましょう。正解というものはありません。次の授業でプレゼンをしてもいいでしょう、エッセーを英語で書いてもいいでしょう。知を探求し発信するためのパートです。

Words in Action

　皆さんの英語を活性化させ、英語をアクティブに使いこなすためのセクションです。本文中で使われている単語や語句表現、あるいは本文そのものを使って、英語が実際に使えるようになるためのノウハウや簡単にできる練習方法を紹介しています。

Further Thinking

1. Consider the wisdom learned from nature, the elderly, or living in foreign countries. Are they similar to the wisdom we find in Japan?
2. Which quotation (by Saint-Exupéry) do you like best? How does it make you feel?
   - A goal without a plan is just a wish.
   - All grown-ups were once children ... but only few of them remember it.
   - It is only with the heart that one can see rightly; what is essential is invisible to the eye.

Words in Action

「人の言ったことを伝える」

　私たちは、人の言ったことを別の人に伝えるということをよく行います。本文中にも、以下のような例が出ています。

People often say that life is like climbing a mountain.
He argues that life is really more like a desert ...
Donahue suggests several ways to cross the desert wisely ...
... Antoine de Saint-Exupery once said, "I stayed up all night ..."

　細い下線部はそれを言った人、太い下線部の動詞はその言い方、二重下線部はその人が言った内容です。最後の例では、引用符が使われているので、このように実際言ったのだということを示しています。以下の例では、言い方がadviceという名詞で示され、その助言の内容がthat節内で示されています。

The advice that one should deflate a tire when caught in sand is very interesting.

　私たちは先人の言ったことを集めて教訓や教えとしたり、関係する人の言ったことを引用して報告をしたり、議論をしたりします。小さな子供が、お母さんがお昼だって、とお兄さんに言うのもそうですし、新聞で総理大臣の失言や発言を取り上げるのも同じ言語の使い方です。

　このような言葉の使い方でよく出てくる動詞としては、

- say、tell、talk、state、inform、express、mention、report、ask、question
- answer、reply、deny、advise、suggest、claim、argue、discuss、explain
- complain、propose、promise、shout、cry、whisper

などがあります。これらの語を使いこなすことで、どのような目的で、どういう言い方で言ったのかをより正確に伝えることができます。

Desert Wisdom / The Power of Friendship from "Korea JoongAng Daily READING Spectrum"
Copyright©2017 Reprinted with permission of Jonghap Books.

Cell Phone Culture: How cultural differences affect mobile use
By Naomi Canton for CNN, September 28, 2012

Men are from Mars, Women are from Venus
Excerpt from "MEN ARE FROM MARS, WOMEN ARE FROM VENUS" by John Gray (pp. 61 - 63).
Copyright 1992 by John Gray. Reprinted with permission of HarperCollins Publishers.

The Beginning Part of Botchan
講談社英語文庫『坊ちゃん』 アラン・ターニー訳

Fuji-san (3,776m)
One Hundred Mountains of Japan by Kyuya Fukada, translated by Martin Hood. Reprinted by permission of University of Hawai'i Press.
Original Japanese version ©1964 Kyuya Fukada. English translation ©2015 Martin Hood.

Malala Yousafzai Nobel Peace Prize Lecture
©The Nobel Foundation (2014) http://nobelprize.org

Emotional Robots
Excerpt(s) from PHYSICS OF THE FUTURE: HOW SCIENCE WILL SHAPE HUMAN DESTINY AND OUR DAILY LIVES BY THE YEAR 2100 by Michio Kaku, copyright © 2011 by Michio Kaku. Used by permission of Doubleday, an imprint of the Knopf Doubleday Publishing Group, a division of Penguin Random House LLC. All rights reserved.

Guernica/ The Art of Lying/ The Three Secrets to Persuasion: Aristotle and Ethos, Pathos, and Logos/ Eating Disorders/ Working Conditions, Death from Overwork/ Maslow's Hierarchy of Needs
Written by Brian Howell

Guernica
Sources: https://en.wikipedia.org/wiki/Guernica_(Picasso)
           https://www.youtube.com/watch?v=l_VSixma864&frags=pl%2Cwn

The Art of Lying
Sources: https://forum.wordreference.com/threads/black-lie.405939/
           http://changingminds.org/explanations/behaviors/lying/four_lies.htm
           https://answers.yahoo.com/question/index?qid=20080215002348AAF2aZp
           http://www.oed.com/view/Entry/108036

The Three Secrets to Persuasion: Aristotle and Ethos, Pathos, and Logos
Sources: https://plato.stanford.edu/entries/aristotle-rhetoric/#means
           https://plato.stanford.edu/entries/aristotle-rhetoric/#means
           https://en.wikipedia.org/wiki/Modes_of_persuasion
           http://www.bizcommunity.com/Article/196/18/123643.html

Eating Disorders
Sources: https://en.wikipedia.org/wiki/Eating_disorder
           https://www.nimh.nih.gov/health/topics/eating-disorders/index.shtml

Working Conditions, Death from Overwork
Sources: http://nordic.businessinsider.com/what-is-karoshi-japanese-word-for-death-by-overwork-2017-10
           https://en.wikipedia.org/wiki/Karōshi
           https://www.usatoday.com/story/news/world/2017/10/06/japan-struggles-karoshi-death-overwork-after-deaths-2-young-women/738915001/
           https://en.wikipedia.org/wiki/Work–life_balance#frb-inline
           http://www.economist.com/node/10329261
           https://web.archive.org/web/20100211031629/http://www.iol.co.za/index.php?set_id=1&click_id=117&art_id=nw20070517081239240C435666
           https://en.wikipedia.org/wiki/War_reparations#World_War_II_Germany Accessed 02.0318:
           https://www.usatoday.com/story/news/world/2016/10/07/japanese-employees-overwork/91726182/

Maslow's Hierarchy of Needs
Sources: Maslow's Hierachy of Needs, Pierre Pichère, 50Minutes.com
           https://www.simplypsychology.org/maslow.html
           https://en.wikipedia.org/wiki/Maslow%27s_hierarchy_of_needs

Unit 1
Desert Wisdom

istock.com / jon11

Let's Chat

1. Who do you think is riding in the car and where do you think it's heading?

2. Would you prefer climbing a high mountain or crossing a vast desert? Why?

Desert Wisdom

People often say that life is like climbing a mountain. Until you reach the top, there are all kinds of difficulties and troubles, and the hardest thing can be coming down from the mountain. Canadian adventurer and consultant Steve Donahue is opposed to this notion. He argues that life is really more like a desert; mountains offer a clear goal, the summit, but deserts are trackless, and people don't know for sure where to go. Donahue suggests several ways to cross the desert wisely, based on his experience.

The most important thing is to follow the compass, not the map. Do not cling to the place where you are but be aware of where you are heading. Mountains and maps have something in common — both have a clear goal and known paths and you can calculate the time to your destination. But unlike mountains, deserts usually don't have roads. Common sense is not enough and no one knows where a path may lead. Therefore, in a desert it is important to read the compass within yourself and pay heed to your own sense of direction rather than what you see. French author and pilot Antoine de Saint-Exupéry once said, "I stayed up all night reading the map. However, it was useless. I couldn't find out where I was."

Notes

l. 1 **Until ...**　〜（する、になる）まで
l. 3 **consultant**　顧問、専門分野における相談相手
l. 4 **is opposed to ...**　〜に反対する／**notion**　考え、考え方
l. 5 **a clear goal, the summit**　明確な目的地すなわち頂上（挿入句）／**trackless**　道のない
l. 8 **the compass**　羅針盤、磁石
l. 9 **cling to**　執着する、固執する／**be aware of ...**　〜に気がつく
l. 11 **destination**　目的地
l. 12 **Common sense**　思慮分別、良識
l. 14 **read**　（地図や羅針盤などを）見て理解する／**pay heed to**　心にとめる、留意する／**your own sense of direction**　自分自身の方向感覚
l. 15 **Antoine de Saint-Exupéry**　アントワーヌ・ド・サン＝テグジュペリ（1900年〜1944年）『星の王子様』などの作品があるフランスの作家、飛行操縦士

④ The advice that one should deflate a tire when caught in sand is very interesting. In the wilderness of the desert, the more you press on the gas to speed up the car, the deeper the car sinks into the sand. A strong ego is important, as is a powerful engine in a car, but when you are in trouble, wisdom dictates letting some air out of the ego. By letting go of past behaviors and beliefs and becoming more humble, you are able to accept the fact that you are not perfect.

⑤ Resting once in a while when you come across an oasis is another wise thing to do. Don't just drink water from the oasis, but rest. Rather than pressing to reach the goal, resting once in a while, restoring your energy and looking both forward and back allows you to work more efficiently. The more you rest, the farther you can get ahead; it's another wisdom of a desert journey.

(382 words)

Notes

l. 18　**deflate**　（タイヤなどから）空気を抜く／**caught in sand**　砂地にはまる
l. 19　**wilderness**　果てしない広がり／**the more ..., the deeper ...**　〜すればするほどさらに深く〜／
　　　press on the gas　アクセルを踏む
l. 20　**A strong ego**　強い自意識、強い自我
l. 22　**dictates**　決定する、支配する／**By letting go of ...**　〜を排除する、〜を一旦忘れる
l. 25　**once in a while**　時々／**come across**　遭遇する、見つける
l. 27　**restoring**　活力を取り戻す
l. 28　**The more ..., the farther ...**　もっと〜すればもっと遠くに

Graphic Organizer

Life as a Desert

Adventurer Steve Donahue argues that **1.** _____ is like a desert.

⬇

Reason
Mountains offer a clear **2.** _____ , but deserts are **3.** _____ and people do not know where they are heading.

Ways to Cross the Desert (Live Life) Wisely

Tip 1

Follow the compass, not the **4.** _____ .

▶ Deserts do not have **5.** _____ , so read the compass within yourself and pay heed to your own sense of **6.** _____ .

Tip 2

7. _____ a tire when caught in sand.

▶ When you are in trouble, let some **8.** _____ out of the ego and become more **9.** _____ .

Tip 3

Rest when you come across an **10.** _____ .

▶ Restoring your **11.** _____ and looking both forward and back allows you to work more **12.** _____ .

Active Learning

1. Listening Task

前置詞や副詞を伴う動詞（句動詞）を本文からみつけて書き出そう。次にこれらの句動詞から３つ選び、正しい短文を作って紹介しあおう。

come _____   oppose _____   based _____
cling _____   be aware _____   pay heed _____
stay _____   find _____   come _____
speed _____   sink _____   get _____

1. _____
2. _____
3. _____

2. Map Task

同じ地図を手元に道順を教える人と、道順を聞いて進む人に分かれます。お互いの地図を見ないで、道順を教える人は宝の在り処を決めた場所に相手を誘導しよう。地図に山や川や小屋などの目印を自由に描き込んで教えあおう。

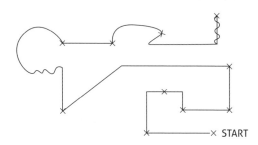

例）Go this way for a couple of minutes until you see the big forest on your left. Then turn left and go on for about 5 minutes until you see a cottage and monument right across from each other.

Tips　道案内をするとき、このような表現が使えます。

You will see a large ---- on the right.　　　You will pass a -----.
It's across from the old mill.　　　　　　　It's on + street name
It's opposite　　　　　　It's near　　　　It's around the corner from
Turn right at the next street　　　　　　　Go one more block. Then turn right.
At the next traffic lights turn ...　　　　　It's going to be on your right.

● Expressions for This Unit

to the North, South, East, West   Go + direction (right, left, down, up, through)
take + road name   turn + right/left   It's on the left/right.
go straight ahead   go straight on   when you get to ...

Further Thinking

1. Consider the wisdom learned from nature, the elderly, or living in foreign countries. Are they similar to the wisdom we find in Japan?
2. Which quotation (by Saint-Exupéry) do you like best? How does it make you feel?
   ・A goal without a plan is just a wish.
   ・All grown-ups were once children ... but only few of them remember it.
   ・It is only with the heart that one can see rightly; what is essential is invisible to the eye.

Words in Action

「人の言ったことを伝える」

　私たちは、人の言ったことを別の人に伝えるということをよく行います。本文中にも、以下のような例が出ています。

　　People often say that life is like climbing a mountain.
　　He argues that life is really more like a desert ...
　　Donahue suggests several ways to cross the desert wisely ...
　　... Antoine de Saint-Exupery once said, "I stayed up all night ..."

　細い下線部はそれを言った人、太い下線部の動詞はその言い方、二重下線部はその人が言った内容です。最後の例では、引用符が使われているので、このように実際言ったのだということを示しています。以下の例では、言い方がadviceという名詞で示され、その助言の内容がthat節内で示されています。

　　The advice that one should deflate a tire when caught in sand is very interesting.

　私たちは先人の言ったことを集めて教訓や教えとしたり、関係する人の言ったことを引用して報告をしたり、議論をしたりします。小さな子供が、お母さんがお昼だって、とお兄さんに言うのもそうですし、新聞で総理大臣の失言や発言を取り上げるのも同じ言語の使い方です。

　このような言葉の使い方でよく出てくる動詞としては、

　　・say、tell、talk、state、inform、express、mention、report、ask、question
　　・answer、reply、deny、advise、suggest、claim、argue、discuss、explain
　　・complain、propose、promise、shout、cry、whisper

などがあります。これらの語を使いこなすことで、どのような目的で、どういう言い方で言ったのかをより正確に伝えることができます。

Unit 2 — The Power of Friendship

Shutterstock/アフロ

Let's Chat

1. Do you know who this man is? What kind of person do you think he is?

2. What can you do to maintain lifelong friendship?

The Power of Friendship

Hollywood actor Robin Williams is known to have a "thousand voices." In the movie "Hook," he played Peter Pan with a young boy's voice and in "Aladdin," he voiced the "Genie" of the lamp in a young woman's voice. In "Mrs. Doubtfire," he was able to reproduce an old British lady's coy ways of speech amazingly. Furthermore, in the movie "Bicentennial Man," his was the voice of a robot. His skill in imitating various voices and expressions makes one forget about any differences of sex and age.

There is a sad story behind how Mr. Williams became so talented at different voices. He was overweight during his childhood. Kids his age made fun of him and no one would play with him. Moreover, he was also lonely at home because of being an only child. So he used make up imaginary friends and create their voices by himself. This later became the base for his voice acting. Was he lonely with just imaginary friends? Or did he long for a real friend? In his early twenties, during his days at the Juilliard School studying drama, he and Christopher Reeve were roommates. The two shared a long friendship that was so sincere they were known as "soul mates."

Mr. Reeve, who became famous as "Superman," was paralyzed from the neck down due to a horse-riding accident in 1995, at the age of 43. When he first lost his laughter in the face of his tragedy, a man came to visit him in hospital. The man, in a funny yellow gown, a surgeon's cap and mask, came

Notes

- l. 4 **reproduce** 再現する、同じような口調で話す / **coy** はにかんだ、恥ずかしがった
- l. 8 **talented** 才能がある
- l. 9 **Kids his age** 彼と同じ年頃の子供たち / **made fun of ...** 〜をからかう
- l. 11 **make up imaginary** 作られた、想像上の
- l. 12 **voice acting** 声の演技
- l. 13 **long for** 切望する、強く望む
- l. 16 **soul mates** 魂の友
- l. 17 **was paralyzed** 麻痺した、不随になった / **from the neck down** 首から下
- l. 19 **in the face of** 直面して
- l. 20 **surgeon's cap** 外科医の帽子

into the ward and talked nonsense in a Russian accent. Mr. Reeve laughed for the first time since the accident because the man's appearance and words were so funny. That moment, the man took off his mask and revealed his face. It was Mr. Williams. To bring laughter to his friend at a difficult time, he practiced all night to perform for just one person. Mr. Reeve later recalled this moment and said, "When seeing my friend, who put a lot of effort in trying to make me laugh, I felt my life will go well."

However, Mr. Reeve died in October 2004 and his wife Dana Reeve followed him on March 6 this year due to lung cancer. Their thirteen-year-old son, Will, became an orphan whom Mr. Williams is now taking care of. Mr. Williams, who has been married twice, has a twenty-year-old son from his former marriage and a seventeen-year-old daughter and fourteen-year-old son with his current wife. Money isn't a big deal for him but it can't have been easy for someone to decide to raise someone else's child. But the power of friendship is strong. An American Indian proverb says, "Friends are those who carry my sorrow on their back."

(468 words)

Notes

l. 21 **ward** 病室
l. 23 **That moment** まさにそのとき／ **revealed** あらわにした、見せた
l. 27 **go well** うまく行く、順調に行く
l. 29 **lung cancer** 肺がん
l. 30 **orphan** 孤児
l. 33 **a big deal** 大変なこと
l. 35 **proverb** ことわざ

Graphic Organizer

Robin Williams' Best Friend

Robin Williams
Hollywood actor who is known to have a "**1.**_____ voices" (e.g. voices of a young boy, a young woman, an British old lady, and a **2.**_____).

During His Childhood
▶ He was lonely, so he made up **3.**_____ friends and created their **4.**_____.
▶ He became skillful in **5.**_____ various voices and expressions.

In His Twenties

▶ He met his "**6.**_____ mate" Christopher Reeve who became famous as "**7.**_____."

In **8.**_____
▶ Mr. Reeve became **9.**_____ in an accident and lost his laughter.
▶ Mr. Williams used his talent to bring laughter to his friend.

In 2004
▶ Mr. Reeve died and his wife **10.**_____ him soon after.
▶ Mr. Williams decided to take care of their **11.**_____, Will.

Robin Williams and Christopher Reeve's **12.**_____ was strong.

Active Learning

1. Information Gap

あなたの友達はどんな人ですか？ お互いに紹介し合おう。

What do you know about your friends?

_____ and I have been friends for about _____ years. (who and how long?)

We met _____. (where?)   He / She likes _____. (what?)

What is your friend like?

He / She has _____. (appearance)

He / She is _____. (character)

2. Prioritizing Task

Friendship（友情）に関する4つのQuestionsについて、あなたの考えに一番近いものをOpinionsの中から選んでみよう。つぎに、Opinionsの中で1から4まで優先順位の番号をふり、あなたと価値観が近い人をクラスの中から探してみよう。

Questions	Opinions
1. How do you meet new friends?	( ) Make friends through other friends. ( ) Make an effort to know co-workers. ( ) Join some clubs, circles or sports teams. ( ) Sign up for Meetup.
2. What are good friends?	Good friends ... ( ) are with you in good times and bad. ( ) are loyal and accept you even when you are in trouble. ( ) will tell you what you need to hear, even if you don't want to hear it. ( ) and you are on the same wavelength.
3. How do you choose a friend?	Choose friends ... ( ) with similar values, interests or goals. ( ) who can take your life/career to the next level. ( ) who have different strengths and weakness from yours. ( ) who offer a listening ear and encourage you.
4. How do you determine a fake friend?	( ) They talk about you behind your back. ( ) They use you to get close to someone you are close to. ( ) They only talk to you when they need something. ( ) They copy your work or use your intelligence.

Tips 意見を尋ねる、賛同を求める、自分の考えを述べるとき、このような表現が使えます。

What do you think about that?   How do you feel about ...?
Do you have any particular views on ...?   From my point of view, ...
It seems to me ...   I'd just like to say ...
I don't think that's so important.   But don't you think ...?

● Expressions for This Unit

Appearance: tall   short   slim   fat   thin   short/ long hair   straight / curly hair   dark hair   handsome   beautiful   old   young

Character: outgoing   sociable   confident   clever   fair   funny   shy   chatty   quiet   determined   dark   optimistic   pessimistic   vulnerable   complicated   witty   kind   obedient   nasty

Further Thinking

1. Introduce any other films and books with the theme of friendship that you would like to recommend.
2. According to a recent study, we are facing a loneliness epidemic, although another study found that investing in close relationships was associated with better health, happiness and well-being in adulthood. How do you see the issue and how would you try to tackle it?

Words in Action

「単語の数え方：活用形と派生形」

　write、writes、wrote、written、writing は何語と数えるでしょうか。1語と言う人もいるでしょうし、5語と言う人もいるでしょう。1語と言う人は、これらの語は動詞の write が変化した語なので、write でまとめて1語と数えたと言うでしょう。5語と言う人は、どれも形が違うので5語としたと言うでしょう。どちらも正しい数え方です。同じようなことが、egg、eggs や slow、slower などにも言えます。これらは名詞や形容詞が変化した形です。では、slow、slowly はどうでしょうか。これらは同じような意味でも、品詞が形容詞と副詞と別になっています。

　では実際の英語ではどのようになっているのでしょうか。本文の第1パラグラフを見てみましょう。actor は「演ずる」という意味の動詞 act に -or を付けて、「演ずる人、役者」という意味の名詞にして使っています。is はもちろん be 動詞が変化した形です。known は know を過去分詞にして使っています。voices は voice を複数形にしたものです。movie は moving picture を短くして、関係する物という意味の -ie を最後に付けたものです。played はもちろん動詞 play に -ed を付けたものです。voiced は名詞の voice の形を変えずにそのまま動詞として、-ed を付けて使っているものです。面白いのは amazingly です。この語は、「驚かす」という意味の動詞 amaze に -ing を付けて形容詞にし、さらに副詞を作る -ly を付けて amazingly として使っています。

　このように英語では1つの語にいろいろなもの（接辞といいます）を付けて、文法的な役割を変えたり、別の品詞に変えて、いろいろな語を作って使っています。中心となる語の意味と、これらの接辞の意味や役割を理解していれば、知っている語の数が何倍にも広がります。

　以下の語はどういう意味の語にどういう接辞が付いてどういう意味や役割で使われている語でしょうか。考えてみてください。

　　　Americanization　　unidentifiable　　enlargement　　antiglobalism

Unit 3
Cell Phone Culture: How Cultural Differences Affect Mobile Use

iStock.com/santypan

Let's Chat

1. Where do you think this woman is? Who do you think she is talking to?

2. When do you feel uncomfortable talking on the phone in public?

Cell Phone Culture: How Cultural Differences Affect Mobile Use

It is a device that three quarters of the world's inhabitants have access to, according to the World Bank, but the etiquette of how to use it differs starkly across cultures.

In Japan, train commuters receive a barrage of recorded announcements telling them to switch their mobiles to silent or vibrate, referred to as "manner mode". Using a mobile in public is frowned upon in a land where collective needs are put above the individual's. "Japanese culture highly values social harmony and social disturbance is heavily sanctioned," explains Satomi Sugiyama, associate professor at Franklin College Switzerland.

If someone tries to board a bus while taking a call, the driver will not let them on, adds cultural anthropologist Mizuko Ito. "In Japan your phone shouldn't be a nuisance to others," she says. "This means generally keeping it on manner mode when out of the house, and not taking calls in cafes and restaurants. If somebody's phone rings, they will be flustered and silence it or take a very quick call," Ito explains. The density of urban spaces, the high use of public transportation, and the relative lack of privacy in homes contribute to ways of communicating that don't impose on others, she explains. Texting, mobile email, games and novels are more popular than voice calls among the Japanese.

Notes
Title mobile 携帯電話
l. 1   device 道具、機器／ three quarters 4分の3／ inhabitants 住民
l. 2   the World Bank 世界銀行／ starkly はっきりと、際立って
l. 4   barrage 集中砲火
l. 6   is frowned upon 認められていない／ collective needs 集団の必要
l. 7   highly values 非常に重要視する
l. 8   heavily sanctioned 重く処罰される
l. 11 cultural anthropologist 文化人類学者
l. 12 a nuisance 迷惑
l. 14 be flustered 狼狽する

In Spain and Italy, in contrast, mobiles are used everywhere and people are not averse to discussing their personal lives in public. Renfe, the state-owned train operating company in Spain, once promoted its journeys on a poster depicting conversations people can have with their partners on cell phones from the train.

The Spanish, like the Italians, happily answer calls in restaurants, during business meetings, conferences and even sometimes during concerts. Discreetly texting or instant messaging under the table during meetings is also commonplace, Amparo Lasén, professor of sociology at the University Complutense de Madrid, says. Spanish people have always discussed their private lives in the streets, so doing so on mobile is just an evolution of that. "Sometimes Spanish people leave movie theaters just to check what is happening on their phone," Lasén says. "You have an obligation to be available to close friends, colleagues and customers. There is an obligation of accountability," she adds.

 Technologies tend to be global. Yet, the ways in which mobile phones are used reflect the cultural differences of how people communicate around the world.

(398 words)

Notes

l. 15　**take a very quick call**　極めて短時間で電話にでる／ **density**　密度、密集
l. 16　**contribute to ...**　〜に貢献する
l. 17　**impose on others**　他人に迷惑を掛ける

l. 20　**are not averse to**　嫌いではない
l. 23　**depicting**　描く
l. 27　**Discreetly texting**　こっそりとメールを出す
l. 30　**evolution**　発展、延長
l. 33　**obligation of accountability**　説明責任

Graphic Organizer

Cell Phone Culture

The etiquette of how to use cell phones **1.** _____ across cultures.

Japan

[Etiquette]
- People **2.** _____ their mobiles to "manner mode" on trains.
- People **3.** _____ mobiles or take a quick call in cafes and restaurants.
- Texting, mobile email, etc. are more **4.** _____ than voice calls.

[Cultural background]
- Collective needs are put **8.** _____ the individual's.
- Social harmony is valued and social **9.** _____ is sanctioned.
- Urban spaces are dense and public **10.** _____ is highly used.

Spain (& Italy)

[Etiquette]
- Mobiles are used **5.** _____.
- Talking on the phone on trains is promoted.
- People happily answer calls in restaurants, **6.** _____ business meetings and concerts.
- Discreetly **7.** _____ during meetings is common.

[Cultural background]
- People have always discussed their private lives in the **11.** _____.
- People feel obligated to be **12.** _____ to close friends, colleagues and customers.

Active Learning

1. Opinion Exchange

海外メディアで報道されたニュースのヘッドライン（a.b）から、日本人の公共マナーについてどんなことを考えますか？自由に意見を交換しあおう。

a) 'World Cup: Japan fans impress by cleaning up stadium' (BBC: 20 June 2018)
b) 'Japanese women asked not to apply make-up during their commute on the train' (The Telegraph, 28 October 2016)

Tips 意見に賛同するとき、しないときに、このような表現が使えます。

Do you think ... is a good idea?　　Are you for ...?　　　　　　... is very good.
... is absolutely right.　　　　　I'm not sure, but I think ...　It's wrong to ...
I would find it difficult to recommend ...　　I'm very much in favor of that

2. Dictogloss

読み上げられた文（1～8）を聴き、文章を再現しよう。それぞれの文を何回か聴き、最初は各自で文章を書き起こし、そのあとグループで協力し合って全部の会話を間違いなく記録してみよう。

1. _____
2. _____
3. _____
4. _____
5. _____
6. _____
7. _____
8. _____

Further Thinking

1. Have you ever experienced another culture? What did you find challenging?
2. What kind of cultural problems do foreign workers face in Japan?

Words in Action

「単語同士の相性：コロケーション」

　人間同士にも仲のいい人同士と、折り合いの悪い人同士がいますが、単語の世界も同様です。以下のような引用が本文中にあります。

> "Japanese culture <u>highly values</u> social harmony and social disturbance is <u>heavily sanctioned</u>."

highly が values を heavily が sanctioned を前から修飾していますが、これを反対にして heavily values や highly sanctioned とは言いません。このようにどのような副詞がどのような語を修飾するのかはおおよそ決まっています。highly という副詞は high という形容詞から派生したものですが、この語がよく修飾する語としては、value 以外に、successful、significant、effective、complex、desirable、intelligent といった形容詞や、skilled、developed、regarded、trained、qualified、recommended、respected、sophisticated などの -ed 形で終わる語もあります。反対に、重いという形容詞 heavy から派生した heavily がよく修飾する語としては、involved、dependent、influenced、armed、populated、criticized、indebted、weighted、criticized、taxed、polluted、defeated、contaminated など、highly と反対に余りいい印象の語ではありません。

　よく big と large、small と little はどう違うのかと聞かれますが、基本的な意味はそれぞれ同じですが、一緒に使われる語が随分と違います。

big： man、house、business、city、thing、difference、name、problem、day
little： girl、boy、thing、one、man、room、house、child、town、piece
large： number、amount、part、scale、area、quantity、proportion、extent
small： number、amount、group、business、town、firm、proportion、boy

big と little は物の大小を言うときによく使われますが、large と small は数量や程度の多い少ないなどを言うときに使われることが分かります。このような言葉同士の関係を知っておくと、使う英語がより自然になり、読んだり聞いたりするときも次にどのような語が来るのかを予測することも可能になります。

Unit 4
Men are from Mars, Women are from Venus

iStock.com/AntonioGuillem

Let's Chat

1. What do you think the woman is saying to the man?

2. Do you have difficulty understanding the opposite sex?

Men are from Mars, Women are from Venus

Expressing feelings versus expressing information

Men and women seldom mean the same things even when they use the same words. For example, when a woman says "I feel like you never listen," she does not expect the word never to be taken literally. Using the word never is just a way of expressing the frustration she is feeling at the moment. It is not to be taken as if it were factual information.

To fully express their feelings, women assume poetic license and use various superlatives, metaphors, and generalizations. Men mistakenly take these expressions literally. Because they misunderstand the intended meaning, they commonly react in an unsupportive manner. In the following chart ten complaints easily misinterpreted are listed, as well as how a man might respond unsupportively.

Notes

Title **Mars** 火星／**Venus** 金星
l. 4　**be taken** 理解される、(意味を) 取られる／**literally** 文字通りに
l. 7　**assume ...** 〜だと思い込む／**poetic license** 詩人のような自由奔放さ
l. 8　**superlatives** 最上級／**metaphors** 比喩 (的な表現)／**mistakenly** 誤って
l. 10　**in an unsupportive manner** 非協力的な態度で
l. 11　**complaints** 文句、不平不満

TEN COMMON COMPLAINTS THAT ARE EASILY MISINTERPRETED

Women say things like this	Men respond like this
"We never go out."	"That's not true. We went out last week."
"Everyone ignores me."	"I'm sure some people notice you."
"I am so tired. I can't do anything."	"That's ridiculous. You are not helpless."
"I want to forget everything."	"If you don't like your job, then quit."
"The house is always a mess."	"It's not always a mess."
"No one listens to me anymore."	"But I am listening to you right now."
"Nothing is working."	"Are you saying it is my fault?"
"You don't love me anymore."	"Of course I do. That's why I'm here."
"We are always in a hurry."	"We are not. Friday we were relaxed."
"I want more romance."	"Are you saying I am not romantic?"

You can see how a "literal" translation of a woman's words could easily mislead a man who is used to using speech as a means of conveying only facts and information. We can also see how a man's responses might lead to an argument. Unclear and unloving communication is the biggest problem in relationships. The number one complaint women have in relationships is: "I don't feel heard." Even this complaint is misunderstood and misinterpreted!

(343 words)

Notes

l. 17 **ridiculous**　ばかげている
l. 19 **a mess**　散らかっている状態
l. 26 **mislead**　誤って理解させる、誤解させる／**conveying**　伝える、伝達する

Graphic Organizer

Problem in Relationships

Women

We **1.** _____ go out.

Women often assume
2. _____ license when
they express their **3.** _____.

They use **4.** _____,
metaphors and generalizations.

They do not expect the words to be
taken **5.** _____.

Men

That's not
6. _____.
We went out
last week.

Men are used to using speech to
convey **7.** _____ and
information.

They take women's words literally
and **8.** _____
the **9.** _____ meaning.

Men commonly react in an
10. _____ manner.

As a result…

He's
unloving…

She's
unclear…

Women do not feel they
are **11.** _____.

Men's responses might
12. _____ to arguments.

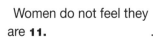

Active Learning

1. Listing Task

主観的な表現である形容詞と客観的な事実を述べる形容詞を本文から見つけて〇で囲もう。つぎに、名詞を修飾する形容詞を使って、矢印が示す描写する順序に従い、身近なものを紹介しあおう。

Easy to change → → → → → More difficult to change

Opinion	Size ⇨ Shape ⇨ Age ⇨ Color	Origin	Material

例）We live in a modern, 8-story, old, concrete building.
　　I like this convenient, small, new, Japanese, laptop.

◆ We saw a _____ .

◆ I have some _____ .

2. Role Play

共働き家族の親であるあなたは、配偶者の家事分担が少ないと思っています。頻度を表す副詞表現を使用しながら相手と話し合って、1週間の家事分担を決めよう。

☐ discipline children　　　　　　　　☐ do house cleaning
☐ wash dishes　　　　　　　　　　　☐ take children to and from a nursery school
☐ cook　　　　　　　　　　　　　　☐ shop for food
☐ take out the garbage　　　　　　　☐ look after the children at home
☐ socialize with neighborhood parents　☐ others

Weekly Schedule

	Mon.	Tue.	Wed.	Thurs.	Fri.	Sat.	Sun.
I							
You							

Tips　優先権　自分の好みを伝え、相手の好みと調整するとき、このような表現が使えます。
　　Do you prefer ... or ...?　　Would you rather ...?　　We can ... or ... What do you think?
　　I'd prefer ..., (if possible).　　I wouldn't mind ... ing on Sunday.

頻度を表す副詞

Always	100%	I always wash dishes.
Usually	90%	I usually cook.
Generally / Normally	80%	I normally look after the children at home.
Frequently / Often	70%	I often socialize with neighborhood parents.
Sometimes	50%	You sometimes take children to and from a nursery school.
Occasionally	30%	I occasionally cook.
Seldom	10%	You seldom take out the garbage.
Rarely	5%	You rarely shop for food!
Never	0%	You never do house cleaning!

Further Thinking

1. Do you think our typical images of what we should and should not do are influenced by our society and culture? Explain with some examples how we are influenced by them.
2. What significant differences have brain scientists found so far between men and women?

Words in Action

「接辞」

　この課では、mistakenly、misunderstand、misinterpreted、mislead のように、mis-（誤った）という接頭辞（語の最初に着ける接辞）が付いた語や、Unit 2で学習した接尾辞（語の最後に着ける接辞）の -ly を付けて副詞として使っている語も、literally、fully、mistakenly、commonly、easily、unsupportively などが使われています。

　しかし、接辞には今まで見てきたもの以外にも、幾つもの接辞があります。本文中の express や expect は ex- で始まっていますが、この接頭辞は exit（出口）からも推測できるように、「外へ」という意味です。press は、pressure や compress などからでも分かるように、「押しつける」という意味です。express は、「外に押し出す」という意味から、「表現する」という意味になりました。expect の pect は、「見る」という意味の語根（語の中心になる部分）-spect- からきています。spectacle、spectacular、spectator、spectrum、speculate などの他に、inspect（中を見る→調べる）、perspective（しっかりと見る→視点）、respect（振り返ってみる→尊敬する）、suspect（下から見る→疑う）などもありますが、どれも「見る」に関係した spect から派生した語です。

　ちなみに、respect の接頭辞 re- は、「後ろ、反対、再度」などの意味を表し、recall、receive、recognize、recommend、record、recover、recreation、restaurant など数多くの語を作っています。suspect の su(s)- は「下の、副」という意味の接頭辞 sub- の変化したもので、subject、submarine、submit、subscribe、substance、substitute、subway、succeed などの接頭辞となっています。

　translators の trans- は「越える、横切る」という意味ですが、transaction、transborder、transfer、transform、transition、transmit、transoceanic、transport などで使われています。

　単語を接頭辞、語根、接尾辞に分解して学習することで、その語の成り立ちや英語という言語の考え方が分かるだけでなく、新しい語に出会ったときにその語の成り立ちから意味を類推することができますし、語彙力の増強にも大いに役立ちます。

Unit 5 The Beginning Part of *Botchan*

渡辺広史 / アフロ

Let's Chat

1. Do you know any of these characters in *Botchan*?

2. What were you like when you were in elementary school?

The Beginning Part of *Botchan*

Here is the beginning of *Botchan* by Soseki Natsume. The main character Botchan is an innocent and rash boy. The original novel written in Japanese has a rhythmical tone and comical style. Do you think the English translation conveys them well?

Ever since I was a child, my inherent recklessness has brought me nothing but trouble.

Once, when I was at primary school, I jumped out of a second-story window and couldn't walk for a week. Some of you may be wondering why I did such a rash thing. There was no particularly deep reason. It was just that, as I stuck my head out of a second-floor window of the new block, one of my classmates jeered at me and said, "You're always bragging, but I bet you couldn't jump from there. Yah! Sissy!"

When I arrived home on the caretaker's back, my father glared at me and said, "Whoever heard of anyone shaking at knees after only jumping from the second floor?" To which I replied that I'd show him. Next time they wouldn't shake.

A relation of mine had given me a foreign-made penknife, and I was holding up the beautiful blade to show my friends how it caught the sunlight when one of them said, "It shines, all right, but I bet it won't cut."

"What do you mean, won't cut? It'll cut anything," I replied, accepting the challenge.

"All right then, let's see you cut your finger," he demanded.

Notes

l. 2 innocent 無邪気な／rash 向こう見ずな、思慮に欠ける
l. 5 inherent 生まれつきの／recklessness 無謀さ
l. 7 a second-story window 2階の窓
l. 11 jeered at ... 〜をやじる／bragging 自慢する
l. 13 glared at ... 〜をにらみつける
l. 14 Whoever heard of ... 〜を誰が聞いたであろうか（いや、誰もいない）［反語的用法］
l. 17 relation 親戚、親類
l. 18 blade （ナイフの）刃
l. 19 cut 切れる

"A finger? Huh! It'll cut a finger as easy as this." So saying, I cut diagonally into the back of my right thumb. Fortunately, it was a small knife, and the bone was hard, so I still have my thumb. But the scar will be with me for life.

If you walked the twenty paces to the eastern end of our garden, you came to a small vegetable plot on a southern slope, right in the middle of which stood a chestnut tree. This tree meant more to me than life itself. When the nuts were ripe, I would go out the back door as soon as I got up, collect those that lay on the ground, and eat them at school. The west side of the vegetable plot adjoined the garden of the Yamashiroya pawnshop, where there lived a kid of thirteen or fourteen called Kantaro. Kantaro was, of course, a coward. But, in spite of this, he used to climb over the trellis fence and steal the chestnuts.

One evening I hid in the shadow of the gate and caught him at last. Having lost his way of escape, he flung himself at me with all his force. He was about two years older than me and, although he was a coward, he was strong. As he made a sudden lunge at my chest with his flat-crowned head, it skidded off into the sleeve of my kimono. Since this prevented me from using my hand, I swung my arm about blindly. Kantaro's head, trapped in my sleeve, whipped giddily to left and right. Finally, being in pain, he clamped his teeth onto my upper arm inside the sleeve. This hurt, so I pushed him up against the fence and threw him backwards with a leg trip. The ground on the pawnshop side was about six feet lower than the vegetable plot. Kantaro, smashing down half the trellis in the process, fell headfirst back into his own territory and landed with a groan.

(537 words)

Notes

l. 23 **diagonally** 対角線上に、斜めに
l. 25 **scar** 切り傷／**for life** 一生涯にわたり
l. 26 **twenty paces** 20歩
l. 27 **plot** 小区画の土地
l. 28 **chestnut tree** 栗の木
l. 29 **were ripe** （果実や実などが）熟した
l. 31 **adjoined** 隣り合っている／**pawnshop** 質屋
l. 33 **trellis fence** 格子（ツルのある植物を這わせるための格子）
l. 35 **flung himself at ...** ～に向けて自分の体を投げつけた
l. 37 **made a sudden lunge at ...** ～に向かって突然突進した／**flat-crowned head** 横に広くつぶれたような形の頭／**skidded off into ...** ～に滑って入ってきた
l. 39 **whipped giddily** 目がくらむほど激しく動いた
l. 40 **clamped his teeth onto ...** 歯で～を締めつけた
l. 42 **with a leg trip** 足を使ってすくい上げて
l. 44 **fell headfirst back into ...** ～に頭から元の方向に落ちた
l. 45 **with a groan** うめきながら

Graphic Organizer

Botchan's Childhood

Botchan's inherent **1.** _____ brought him lots of troubles.

Fact 1

His **2.** _____ said, "I bet you couldn't jump from the **3.** _____ window."

So he **4.** _____ out and couldn't **5.** _____ for a week.

Fact 2

His friend said "I bet your **6.** _____ won't cut."

So he **7.** _____ the challenge and cut his **8.** _____ .

Fact 3

Kantaro, who was **9.** _____ than him, tried to **10.** _____ chestnuts.

So he **11.** _____ Kantaro and **12.** _____ him to the ground with a leg trip.

Active Learning

1. Information Gap
過去に怪我や傷を負ったことがありますか？情報交換しあおう。

> Have you ever been injured in an accident?

> Yes, I injured my leg when I fell down the stairs.

Tips 怪我や負傷したとき、このような表現が使えます。

injured my leg　　scraped my knee　　burnt my hand　　twisted my ankle
sprained my wrist　　tripped over　　pull a muscle　　tore the ligament in my knee
jammed my finger in ...　　bumped my head　　broke my nail / tooth
dislocated my shoulder　　had cramp in my leg　　had a bruise on my elbow
had muscle ache　　It really hurt!

相手の気の毒な話に相槌を打つときには、このような表現が使えます。
Oh, I'm sorry to hear that.　　That's a pity.　　Oh, that's bad luck.　　I know how it feels.

2. Story Telling
日本昔話の中から一つ話を選び、それをベースに協力してオリジナルの昔話を創作してみよう。グループで順番に一文ずつ作成し、話をつないでいきながら、一つの話を完成させよう。

One summer night,　　One day,　　After ...,　　So,　　Then,　　And finally,
Eventually,　　Just then,　　In the meanwhile,　　To one's surprise,
astonishingly　　somehow

Once upon a time, there lived ...

1. _____
2. _____
3. _____
4. _____
5. _____

Further Thinking

1. Read the beginning part of the original version of *Botchan* in Japanese. Do you like the story? How well does the translated version convey the style of the original?
2. Describe a book you like, give a short presentation about it, and hold a brief classroom discussion on what you have been reading.

Words in Action

「翻訳の難しさ」

　日本の文学作品を英語に訳すのは簡単なことではありません。よく出される例として、川端康成の『雪国』の冒頭の部分の訳があります。「国境の長いトンネルを抜けると雪国であった」この文の主語は列車なのか、あるいは主人公なのか。

　『坊っちゃん』においても、同じような例は幾つもあります。冒頭の、「親譲りの無鉄砲で小供の時から損ばかりしている。」も、英訳は Ever since I was a child, my inherent recklessness has brought me nothing but trouble. であり、直訳すれば「親譲りの無鉄砲が自分に問題ばかりをもたらしている」となるでしょうか。英訳の方が因果関係が日本語よりもはっきりさせていることがわかります。この主語の問題は、すぐ後にも出てきます。「庭を東へ二十歩に行き尽すと、南上がりにいささかばかりの菜園があって、真中に栗の木が一本立っている。」この最初の部分の主語は、敢えて言えば「行き尽す」人でしょうが、誰というものでもないので、書かれていません。英文の主語は、話し手や聞き手を含めた一般の人々を指す you です。真ん中の部分の主語は「菜園」でしょう。しかし英文では引き続き you です。最後の部分は「栗の木」が主語で、この部分は日本文と英文は同じです。

　主語や文構造以外にも、単語表現のレベルでかなりの困難が見受けられます。例えば、「小使」です。これは caretaker と訳されていますが、『広辞苑』（第六版）によれば小使とは「学校・会社・官庁などで雑用に従事する人。用務員」とありますが、Longman Dictionary of Contemporary English (6th ed) では、caretaker を、BrE "someone whose job is to look after a building, especially a school" とあり、『新英和大辞典』（第六版）では、「《英》（公共施設などの）管理人，営繕係《米》janitor)」と記されています。もっと難しいのは、「おれの袷の袖の中にはいった。」でしょうか。「袷の袖」は the sleeve of my kimono と訳されていますが、袷は kimono、袖は sleeve と同じものでしょうか。是非辞書などの記述を参考にして考えてみてください。本来なら違うものを、何とか近似値に近づける苦労が翻訳なのかもしれません。

Unit 6
Guernica

"Guernica"1937, Oil on canvas, 349.3 x 776.6cm, Museo Nacional Centro de Arte Reina Sofia
©2017-Succession Pablo Picasso – SPDA(JAPAN)

Let's Chat

1. What do you think the characters in the picture are saying?

2. Who is your favorite artist? Why?

Guernica

When we look at almost any painting or artwork by Pablo Picasso, probably one of the greatest artists of the twentieth century, we react with confusion. We may be familiar with his other works, but they do not always help us understand his visual puzzles. Picasso's work is not typical or traditional; to help us understand his work, we need to know that the artist is not attempting to make a flat surface have depth. However, he still lets us see many sides and views on this flat surface. How does he do this?

Simply stated, Picasso can be said to walk around his figures and observe them from every angle that he chooses in a real, three-dimensional space. Imagine that you are the painter. In a studio, you can see the back of a person. You can see that person from the side. You can look down on the person from above. Now, on a two-dimensional surface such as that of a painting, this selection of views should not exist together, especially not if it is a realistic illustration. However, Picasso does not care about this. He simply selects the angles or views that are important to him. Some might say that this is a recipe for chaos, and, when we think of his masterpiece, *Guernica*, of 1937, we may indeed at first think that this is exactly the case.

Notes

l. 2   **with confusion**　困惑、混乱しながら
l. 8   **Simply stated**　端的に言えば／**figures**（絵の対象となる）人物
l. 9   **three-dimensional**　3次元の
l. 10 **Imagine that**　～だと想像してみよう
l. 14 **illustration**　描写した物、絵
l. 15 **a recipe for chaos**　混乱の原因
l. 17 **the case**　真実、その通り

Guernica is a painting that makes a protest against the inhumanity of war and the suffering of civilians, most especially of women and children. In 1937 whilst living in Paris, Picasso learned of the bombing of the town of Guernica by General Franco's forces. Picasso set to work painting a huge canvas in blacks, whites, and greys showing the suffering of the inhabitants of this town.

The painting is complex but it is open to varying interpretations. What can we see in the painting? We can make out a number of women. One woman is lamenting the death of her child. We can see an injured horse. We can see part of a bull. We can see the head of a soldier holding a sword, but he has no body. Other objects we can see include a lamp, a window, fire, and an electric light bulb. As in many of his artworks, certain objects, especially eyes, are placed in impossible places. In this way, Picasso shows the complexity of all the events and decisions that led up to this terrible event.

(412 words)

Notes

l. 18 **inhumanity** 残酷さ、残忍さ
l. 20 **learned of ...** 〜を知った
l. 24 **is lamenting** 嘆き悲しんでいる
l. 27 **objects** （描かれている）事物
l. 30 **led up to ...** 〜を引き起こした

Graphic Organizer

Picasso and *Guernica*

Pablo Picasso

- One of the greatest artists of the **1.** _____ century.
- His works are not **2.** _____ or traditional.
- He lets us see many sides and views on a **3.** _____ surface by selecting the angles or views that are **4.** _____ to him.

Guernica (1937)

The painting makes a protest against the **5.** _____ of war and the **6.** _____ of civilians.

Objects in the Painting

women
injured **7.** _____
bull
soldier
lamp
window
fire
electric **8.** _____ bulb

Techniques Used

- Black, white and **9.** _____ are used
→ to show the suffering of the **10.** _____ of Guernica.

- **11.** _____ are placed in impossible places
→ to show the **12.** _____ of events and decisions that led up to the war.

Active Learning

1. Role Play

美術館の学芸員になったつもりで、下の額縁を見立てた図形の位置関係を参考にして、*Guernica* の絵を来訪者役の相手に説明してみよう。

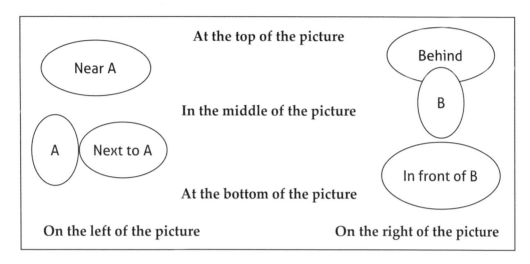

2. Describe a Picture

AとBのどちらの絵が好きですか？それぞれの絵の特徴やメッセージについて、自分の解釈や意見を含めて紹介しよう。また、聞き手の感想も聞きだそう。

A. *The Annunciation* by Leonardo da Vinci (1472-1475)   B. *The Scream* by Edvard Munch (1893)

● Expressions for This Unit

In the picture I can see …	There's / There are …	The people are … -ing
It looks like a …	Maybe it's a …	It might be a …
I find … fascinating.	I'm quite intrigued by …	

【名詞】	canvas	inhabitants	chaos	complexity	inhumanity	Picasso
【動詞】	hold	protest	suffer	injure	imagine	interpret

Further Thinking

1. Select a piece of artwork. Research the story behind the work and give a description to the audience.
2. Create a written argument that supports your interpretation of the artwork. Debate with someone who holds a different view and consider various perspectives.

Words in Action

「区切り読み：意味を考えながら音読する」

　以下に示した文章は、本文の一番最初の文です。これを声に出して読んでみましょう。最初から最後まで一気に読むことは無理でしょうし、意味と言うことを考えれば、どこかで区切って読む必要があることは理解できます。では、どこで区切ればいいでしょうか。ヒントになるのが文の構造と意味です。英語は大体において句が意味のまとまりになっています。名詞句、動詞句、前置詞句、副詞句などで一つの意味の塊を作っています。その意味の塊の境界に２重斜線を引いてみましょう。おそらく、以下のようになるでしょう。

> When we look at//almost any painting or artwork//by Pablo Picasso, //probably one of the greatest artists//of the twentieth century, //we react with confusion.

　look は文法的には自動詞ですが、at と一緒に他動詞のように使われますので、at の後で切ってあります。次の塊はその動詞 look at の目的語に当たる名詞句です。by 以下は「〜によって」という意味の前置詞句です。その後の２つの塊の部分はピカソについての説明を書き加えている部分ですが、長すぎるので artists の後で一旦区切るとよいでしょう。最後の部分はこれで一まとまりです。

　さあ、意味のまとまりを意識しながら、まとまりの最後では声の調子を落として区切りを付けるようにして音読してみましょう。読んでいる本人も、それを聞いている人も意味のまとまりをきちんと理解することができるでしょう。この英語のリズム感は、英語を音読するときだけでなく、英語を黙読するとき、話すとき、聞くとき、書くときにも役に立ちます。残りの本文も意味のまとまりごとに区切り、ペアを組んでお互いに音読をし合ってみましょう。

Unit 7
The Art of Lying

iStock.com/tommasolizzul

Let's Chat

1. In what situation would you wear a mask like this?

2. Is it ever okay to tell a lie?

The Art of Lying

From the earliest age we are taught by our parents and teachers not to lie. We know that it is bad, and when we lie we feel guilty. We see that lying causes stress and confusion in others and after a certain age we realise how damaging or dangerous lying can be. However, our feelings about lying are more complex when we actually lie in real life.

We are aware that we lie for various purposes and with many different intentions. One type of lie is well-known to everyone, and that is a white lie. This kind of lie is told in order to protect someone, usually a family member or a friend, from learning about an uncomfortable truth. We know that if we tell a white lie to someone it will save her from knowledge that would cause her unnecessary pain. For example, your friend might buy a dress that you personally feel does not look attractive. However, when your friend asks you how the dress looks on her, you might say that it looks great in order to spare her embarrassment. This kind of lie might be described as weak and will protect her in the short term.

Notes

l. 2   **feel guilty**   罪の意識を感じる、やましく思う
l. 3   **damaging**   害を及ぼす
l. 7   **intentions**   意図
l. 9   **learning about ...**   〜について知る
l. 10 **save her from knowledge**   彼女が知らないようにする
l. 13 **looks on her**   彼女が着て似合う / **spare her embarrassment**   恥ずかしい思いをせずに済む

At the other extreme, we speak of a black or blatant lie. This type of lie is told in order to hurt someone or to gain an advantage. Unlike in the case of a white lie, it does not take into consideration the feelings of other people. For example, a student in school might falsely accuse another student whom she does not like of stealing her pen or book. In this case, the teller of the lie will cause difficulty for the other student.

Now, in between white and black we of course find grey. We often speak of 'grey areas' in life, referring to a situation that we are uncertain about. In terms of lying, we can imagine that someone might tell a lie because she or he has good intentions. However, this lie might eventually have consequences that could lead to misunderstandings or difficulties which were not intended. As an example, you might want to have a romantic relationship with someone you consider would be a suitable partner. In order to impress that person, you might hint to him that you earn a little more money than you actually do. In the short term, this might cause no problems, but, later on, your partner might learn about your grey lie and feel that you cannot be trusted.

(419 words)

Notes

l. 16　**blatant**　あくどい
l. 18　**take into consideration ...**　〜を考慮しない
l. 19　**falsely**　偽って、虚偽の／**accuse ... of ...**　〜を〜であると非難する、責める
l. 25　**eventually**　結局は、最後には／**consequences**　結果
l. 28　**impress**　よい印象を与える
l. 29　**hint**　ほのめかす

Graphic Organizer

Different Types of Lies

People lie for various **1.** _____ and different intentions.

White lies

- Told to protect someone
- Saves someone from feeling unnecessary **2.** _____
- Protects someone in the **3.** _____ term

[Example]
Tell your friend that she looks **4.** _____ even though you do not think so

Black lies

- Told to **9.** _____ someone or to gain an **10.** _____
- Does not consider other people's **11.** _____

[Example]
Falsely accuse a student you do not like of **12.** _____ your pen

Grey lies

- Told with **5.** _____ intentions but might lead to **6.** _____ or difficulties
- People might feel that you cannot be **7.** _____.

[Example]
Hint a suitable partner that you **8.** _____ more money than you actually do

Active Learning

1. Classifying Task

楽観的 (positive adjectives) と悲観的 (negative adjectives) な形容詞、またどちらでもない形容詞 (neutral) に分類して下の表に書き込もう。

[Adjectives]

scared	surprised	worried	excited	frustrated
relieved	intrigued	pleased	confused	embarrassed
impressed	trusted	nervous	silly	uncomfortable
cheerful	happy	content	uncertain	suspicious
attractive	complex	dangerous	damaging	guilty
painful	stressful	sad		

Positive adjectives	Neutral	Negative adjectives

Tips 形容詞の中には、人をある気持ちにさせる –ing 形と、感情を表す –ed 形とがあります。
例）The movie was really bor<u>ing</u>. We were very bor<u>ed</u>.

2. Two Truths and a Lie

自分について何か3つのこと（2つの真実と1つの嘘）を相手に伝えよう。その際、そのときの自分の気持ちについて形容詞を用いて表現しよう。相手はどれが嘘だったか当ててみよう。どうしてそれが嘘だと思ったのか、その理由も述べてみよう。

This actually happened.

When? _____.

Where? _____.

What happened ? _____.

How did it make you feel? _____.

I will never forget about this _____ happening.

Tips 嬉しい、嫌だ、安堵する気持ちを表すとき、このような表現が使えます。
I'm (very) pleased about …　　I'm very annoyed about …　　… makes me cross (angry)
I can't stand …　　I'm fed up with …　　It's a great relief …　　I'm glad to hear about …

Further Thinking

1. Imagine you had a lie detector. Who would you like to use it against and what would you like to ask?
2. What is "fake news"? Research and explain the problems it causes.

Words in Action

「談話の流れ：文頭と文末の役割」

　言葉はメッセージを伝えるために使われることが多いのですが、その伝え方にはある種の特徴と共通点があります。文の最初の部分では前の文で述べたことを受ける、その文がこれから言おうとしている事柄を予告するような役割を担っています。一方、文の最後は新たな事柄やその詳細について伝えることが一般的です。具体的に本文の第2パラグラフを例に取ってみてゆきましょう。

> We are aware that we lie for various purposes and with many different intentions. One type of lie is well-known to everyone, and that is a white lie. This kind of lie is told in order to protect someone, usually a family member or a friend, from learning about an uncomfortable truth. We know that if we tell a white lie to someone it will save her from knowledge that would cause her unnecessary pain. For example, your friend might buy a dress that you personally feel does not look attractive. However, when your friend asks you how the dress looks on her, you might say that it looks great in order to spare her embarrassment. This kind of lie might be described as weak and will protect her in the short term.

　破線の文頭の部分では、一般的なことや前の文で述べたことを受けた表現となっています。波線の部分はこれから述べることが「例」である、あるいは文の論旨が変わると言うことを予告しています。太線の部分は基本的には文末に当たる部分で、その文が伝えようとしている新しい情報を現しています。二重線の部分は直前の内容の詳細です。

　このように文章全体の流れの大枠が理解できると、この文は「何について」述べ、その結論は「何なのか」、これからどういうことが述べられるのか、この部分は詳細か否か、などを分かった上で文章を読み進められ、読解のスピードが上がり、速読が可能となります。

Unit 8　Fuji-san (3,776m)

iStock.com/kokoroyuki

Let's Chat

1. How does this picture make you feel?

2. What do you think Mt. Fuji is for the Japanese people?

Fuji-san (3,776m)

(48) Every country has its famous mountain. But no other peak represents its country or sums up the spiritual essence of its people as Fuji does. Ever since the *Manyoshu* poet wrote that "its name shall be told through the generations," what a wealth of sentiments Fuji has inspired in us, the Japanese. If the mountain had not existed, our history might have taken a very different course.

(49) The phrase *hachimen-reiro*, meaning "graceful in all its aspects," was coined with Fuji in mind. Its form keeps its beauty whether viewed from north or south, east or west. All other mountains have their quirks, from which they draw their individual charm. But Fuji is simply vast and pure. In fact, I'm tempted to call it magnificently vulgar. Yes, would-be intellectuals might want to say that such starkness is tantamount to vulgarity. In the end, through, we all have to submit to this magnificent vulgarity.

(50) Ike Taiga climbed Fuji more than once, each time by a different route so that he could see it from all directions, from which he created a woodblock print series of one hundred views of Fuji. Hokusai was also a connoisseur of the mountain. Among his *Thirty-Six Views of Fuji*, he handed down to posterity two undoubted masterpieces, the *Red Fuji* (*Gaifu kaisei*) and *Thunderstorm below Mt. Fuji* (*Sanka hakuu*). Muso Kokushi included Fuji in the backdrop to his gardens, while Kitamura Tokoku discovered in the mountain his poetic muse.

Notes

l. 1　**represents**　代表する
l. 2　**sums up**　まとめ上げる／**the spiritual essence**　精神的な神髄、本質
l. 3　**shall ...**　〜することになるであろう
l. 4　**a wealth of sentiments**　豊かな情感／**inspired in us**　私たちに抱かせる、湧き起こす
l. 6　**was coined**　（言葉として）新たに作られた
l. 8　**quirks**　特徴、奇抜さ
l. 9　**vast and pure**　広大で純粋な／**am tempted to ...**　〜する誘惑に駆られる
l. 10　**magnificently vulgar**　すばらしく（見事に）卑俗の／**would-be intellectuals**　知識人志向の人々
l. 11　**starkness**　際立っていること／**tantamount to ...**　〜と同じである／**vulgarity**　卑俗性
l. 12　**submit to ...**　〜に服従する
l. 14　**a woodblock print series**　浮世絵の連作
l. 15　**connoisseur**　専門の鑑定家
l. 16　**posterity**　後世
l. 18　**backdrop**　背景
l. 19　**poetic muse**　詩的なインスピレーション

Today, Fuji is everybody's mountain. It is the butt of jokes, songs, and witticisms. It is worked to death in proverbs and similes. It adorns the front page of every inaugural newspaper edition. Numberless products and their makers appropriate its name.

Fuji is there for everyone and yet, soaring into eternity, stands for something beyond any man's grasp.

(298 words)

Notes
l. 20 **butt**   話題、ネタ
l. 21 **witticisms**   機知／ **is worked to death**   しばしば登場する／ **similes**   直喩／ **adorns**   飾る
l. 22 **inaugural newspaper edition**   新聞の初版
l. 24 **soaring into eternity**   永遠の存在へと昇華する
l. 25 **man's grasp**   人知

Graphic Organizer

Fuji as a Source of Inspiration

- Its form keeps its 1._____ viewed from any angle.
- It is simply vast and 2._____.
- It is magnificently 3._____.

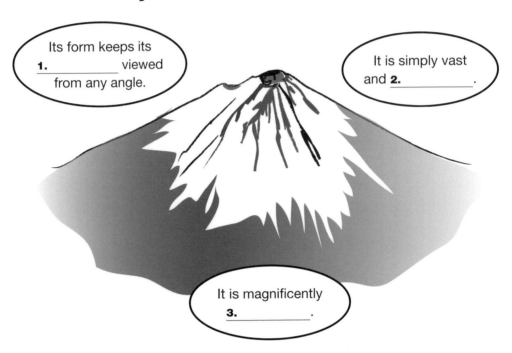

Fuji has inspired the 4._____ over generations.

In the Past

- Ike Taiga and 5._____ created woodblock 6._____ of the views of Fuji.
- Muso Kokushi included Fuji in the 7._____ of his garden.
- Kitamura Tokoku discovered in Fuji his 8._____ muse.

Today

Fuji is used in

- jokes, 9._____ and witticisms.
- proverbs and 10._____.
- 11._____ newspaper edition.
- 12._____ and its names.

Active Learning

1. Opinion Exchange

思い出に残る景色について、感動表現を交えて聞き手に説明しよう。写真がある場合、聞き手は聞いた景色を絵で再現し、実際の写真と照らし合わせてみよう。

Tips 驚きや感動を表すとき、このような表現が使えます。
What a surprise!   That's amazing!   My goodness!   I don't believe it!
Fantastic!   Terrific!   Super!   The scenery was breathtaking!
How marvelous!   ... has a wonderful / splendid/ magnificent view.
It gives me great pleasure/satisfaction to see ...
I can't tell you how delighted I am about ...

2. Decision Making

登山に必要な最小限のサバイバルキットを用意しよう。各自が6個の優先順位をリストアップし、そのあとグループで合意した6品目を挙げよう。遭難救助員が選ぶリストと照らしあわせてポイントをつけ、チームごとに競い合おう。

[Survival kit list]

water	torch/flashlight	knowledge	mental fitness	signal panel
rope	a plastic whistle	first-aid kit	fire cubes	lighter
batteries for headlamp	hypothermia prevention		knife	map & compass

① Item _____   Reason _____
② Item _____   Reason _____
③ Item _____   Reason _____
④ Item _____   Reason _____
⑤ Item _____   Reason _____
⑥ Item _____   Reason _____

● Expressions for This Unit

flowing rivers	lakes	mountain range	streams (narrow paths of water)	
bays	rock cliffs	horizon	farmland	the summit (the peak)
valleys	foothills	woods (small forests)	rolling hills	sandy beaches
rice fields	waterfalls	dramatic	peaceful	spiritual
poetic	vast	inspiring	impressive	lush green
stretch to ...	Shall we ...?	Let's ...	How/What about ...?	Why don't we ...?
May I suggest ...?				

Further Thinking

1. Select a tourist spot you like, make a sightseeing brochure, and present it in a way that will make the audience want to visit.
2. Write notes about a memorable trip you have taken, including the itinerary.

Words in Action

「類義語辞典」

　この課の富士山に関する描写では、一般に使われる表現とは趣が異なる表現が多く使われているようです。例えば、a wealth of sentiments と第1パラグラフにありますが、この wealth という語は「富、財産」という意味ですが、a wealth of ~ と使うことで、「財産ほどの~、多くの~」という意味になります。単に a lot of というよりは優雅に響きます。類義語辞典などを参照にすると、an abundance of、a store of、a treasury of などの他に、a heap of、a pile of、a mountain of、an ocean of、a sea of などの分かりやすい表現も紹介されています。

　第2パラグラフの quirk は「特徴、奇抜さ」という意味ですが、類義語辞典などを引くと、peculiarity、characteristic、trait、feature などの語が掲載されています。また、富士山を But Fuji is simply vast and pure. と描写した部分がありますが、この vast は「広い、広大な」、pure は「純粋な、混ざりけのない」という意味ですが、vast の類義語として huge、broad、wide、boundless、immeasurable、infinite、enormous、gigantic などが紹介されています。もっと簡単な very big、very large、giant などとも掲載されています。magnificently vulgar も面白い表現です。magnificently とは、「壮大に、荘厳に」といった意味の副詞です。一方、vulgar とは、「庶民の、通俗の」という意味から、「洗練されていない、野暮な」という意味もあり、決して品のいい意味ではないのですが、敢えてこの両者と組み合わせることで、富士山の高貴さと庶民性を言い表しているのでしょう。tantamount とは余り使わないイタリア語から来た語ですが、equivalent to、same as と同じような意味です。connoisseur は18世紀にフランス語から来た単語で、「知っている」というのが原義です。expert、specialist、authority などと言い換えてもいいでしょう。

　このように類義語辞典を引くことで、同じような意味の語彙表現をたくさん目にすることができますし、その違いなどを調べるよいきっかけにもなります。類義語辞典は、語彙力の増強にうってつけのツールです。

Unit 9
The Three Secrets to Persuasion:
Aristotle and Ethos, Pathos, and Logos

iStock.com/TMSK

Let's Chat

1. When and where do you think this architecture was built?

2. Are you good at persuading people?

The Three Secrets to Persuasion: Aristotle and Ethos, Pathos, and Logos

The Art of Rhetoric was written by the Greek philosopher and scientist, Aristotle; its origins lie in the fourth century, B.C. It is a collection of notes made by Aristotle from his students' reactions to his lectures. The purpose of his text was to explain the art of persuasion, that is to say, to lead one's audience to agree with the speaker's opinion or argument. The part of the text which deals with persuasion is divided into three clear parts: ethos, pathos, and logos.

Ethos deals with the believability of the speaker, which is to say how much we can believe what the speaker is saying. In order to be believed, the audience needs to trust the speaker. How can this be achieved? There are two ways. In the first case, the audience recognises the authority, education, and experience of the speaker. Thus, if the speaker is a university lecturer, the student will acknowledge that the speaker has authority. However, the speaker must also convince his or her audience with the way that he or she speaks, with the methods that he or she uses to persuade.

Notes

Title Aristotle アリストテレス（前384〜前322）古代ギリシャの哲学者
l. 1　**Art**　技術、〜術／**Rhetoric**　修辞学、説得術
l. 2　**origins**　起源
l. 4　**that is to say**　すなわち、換言すれば
l. 10　**be achieved**　達成される
l. 11　**authority**　権威
l. 13　**acknowledge**　認める、受け入れる
l. 14　**convince**　納得させる、説得する

Pathos deals with the appeal to emotion and imagination. The speaker tries to establish an emotional connection between herself and the audience so that the audience can feel involved. One way to do this is for the speaker to tell stories and use the kind of language and images, including metaphors, which draw out emotional reactions from the audience such as anger, joy, pity, sympathy, love, or laughter. By skillfully using these elements, the speaker will make the audience identify with the speaker's message.

Logos speaks of the appeal to logic and reason. The speaker's message should be clear, concise, and offer evidence to support her message. What kind of evidence can be used in this case? The speaker might use facts, statistics, pictures, the results of studies or surveys, or give examples. If the speaker does not support her talk with any of these kinds of evidence, the audience will probably question her message or not believe her at all.

In today's political climate we might want to step back and study how relevant or useful Aristotle's methods of persuasion still are. Can they still be used in a world where facts and evidence are often ignored or replaced by opinions, where such invented phrases as 'alternate facts' and 'fake news' are often used simply to reject claims which politicians find inconvenient or disagree with?

(414 words)

Notes

l. 17　establish　確立する
l. 18　feel involved　関係があるよう感じる
l. 19　metaphors　比喩
l. 20　pity　残念さ
l. 21　sympathy　同情／ elements　要素
l. 22　identify　同一の物と思う
l. 23　logic　論理／ reason　物の道理、理性
l. 25　statistics　統計
l. 28　question　疑う
l. 29　climate　状況、風潮
l. 30　relevant　妥当な、関連している
l. 31　evidence　証拠／ replaced by ...　～によって取って代わられる
l. 32　alternate facts　「もう一つの事実」／ fake news　「偽ニュース」

Graphic Organizer

The Three Secrets to Persuasion

Written by 1. _____ in his book *The Art of Rhetoric*

	ETHOS	PATHOS	LOGOS
WHAT	Believability of the speaker	Appeal to 2. _____ and imagination	Appeal to 3. _____ and reason
HOW (method)	▶ Make the audience recognize the speaker's 4. _____, education and experience ▶ Convince the audience with the way of 5. _____ and persuading	▶ Tell stories and use language and 6. _____ that draw out the audience's 7. _____ reactions (e.g. anger, joy, and love)	▶ Make the message 8. _____, concise and offer 9. _____ (e.g. facts and statistics) to support the speaker's message
WHY (purpose)	To make the audience 10. _____ the speaker	To make the audience feel involved and 11. _____ with the speaker's message	To make the audience 12. _____ the speaker's message

Active Learning

1. Role Play

人柄（Ethos）、感情（Pathos）、理論（Logos）を2つずつ使って、以下の要求を当事者になったつもりで相手をうまく説得してみよう。どのアプローチならうまく説得できるかを試してみよう。

1. Customer & Staff in a shop
   To market beauty products effectively to many people of all ages
2. Student & Teacher
   To ask your teacher to approve your attendance although you were 35 minutes late for class
3. You & Your friend
   To recommend your friend, who hates keep-fit exercise, to go jogging every day
4. You & Your parents
   To get permission from your parents to study abroad for a year
5. You & the CEO of a big company
   To propose raising a lot of money in a hurry for victims of a disaster
6. You & Your boss in the same company
   To place advertisements on Internet boards warning people not to believe fake news on Instagram

Tips 相手の賛同を引き出したいとき、このような表現が使えます。

(Yes, but) on the other hand ...   Well, think of it this way ...
Yes, but if we look at the whole picture, ...   Can I ..., please?

2. Decision Making

説得術を効果的に使って、ある製品の広告のプランをたててみよう。どんな製品をどんなアプローチで販売したら成功するかプランをたてよう。

Item/ Figure	Ethos (speaker's characters)	Pathos (emotional appeal)	Logos (data / universal truths)

● Expression for This Unit

I'm sure that ...   I'm absolutely certain that ...
I'd do anything for ... (Use tender, half-broken tones in your voice/manner).
It is proven that ...   Statistically,   Experts say ...

The Three Secrets to Persuasion: Aristotle and Ethos, Pathos, and Logos

Further Thinking

1. Find an advertisement that uses ethos, pathos, or logos. Explain how the three elements are used in it.
2. Today, we are living in the era where we get information from apps, blogs and social media that enhance 'fake news', encourage distrust in the 'other' and create a negative attitude towards facts or science. How can we effectively communicate to be understood?

Words in Action

「早読み競争」

　読解力を促進するための方法として、「早読み競争」というのがあります。Unit 9 の本文を使ってやってみましょう。

- ペアを作ります。
- 一人（A）が Unit 9 の本文を 30 秒間音読します。その間、もう一人（B）は、A が音読しているのを聞きながら、本文の同じ部分を黙読してゆきます。
- 30 秒経ったら A は音読をやめて、どこまで音読できたのか印を付けておきます。
- 次に B が A と同じように本文の最初から 30 秒間、音読してゆきます。A は、B がやったように、B が音読しているのを聞きながら、B が音読している部分を黙読してゆきます。
- 30 秒経ったら、B は音読をするのをやめ、どこまで音読できたのか印を付けておきます。
- 同じ事を、A—B、A—B というように、3 回繰り返します。
- 合計で、A と B は同じ本文を最初から 3 回音読し、3 回相手が音読するのを聞きながら黙読したことになります。
- 当然のことながら、A も B も 1 回目よりは 2 回目が、2 回目よりは 3 回目の方が、書いてある内容や英語そのものに慣れていくので、音読で到達した地点が先へ先へと伸びてゆくはずです。

　一般に、音読で読める速さがその人が英文を理解できる速さとほぼ同じであるといわれています。より速く音読できるようになるには、単語のスペリングを見て反応する時間を短くしたり、よく一緒に使われる単語のグループを普段からしっかりと認識しておき、一気に読み込めるようにしたり、意味のまとまりごとに認識して読み込めるようにすることが大切です。そのためには、内容を理解した英文を繰り返し音読することが重要になります。

Unit 10 Malala Yousafzai Nobel Peace Prize Lecture

代表撮影 / ロイター / アフロ

Let's Chat

1. What do you think Malala is telling the audience?

2. How would you feel if you were banned from going to school?

Malala Yousafzai Nobel Peace Prize Lecture

Discrimination against women still exists in the educational sector in many countries. Malala Yousafzai from Pakistan demands that girls be allowed to receive an education. She was shot by the Taliban, but survived and received the 2014 Nobel Peace Prize as the youngest ever winner for her struggle for the right of all children to education. Here is a part of her Nobel lecture.

.... Education is one of the blessings of life—and one of its necessities. That has been my experience during the 17 years of my life. In my paradise home, Swat, I always loved learning and discovering new things. I remember when my friends and I would decorate our hands with henna on special occasions. And instead of drawing flowers and patterns we would paint our hands with mathematical formulas and equations.

We had a thirst for education, ... because our future was right there in that classroom. We would sit and learn and read together. We loved to wear neat and tidy school uniforms and we would sit there with big dreams in our eyes. We wanted to make our parents proud and prove that we could also excel in our studies and achieve those goals, which some people think only boys can.

Notes

l. 1   Discrimination　差別
l. 2   demands　要求する、求める［続く that 節内の動詞は原形を使う］
l. 3   the Taliban　「タリバン」（イスラム主義組織）
l. 4   the Nobel Peace Prize　ノーベル平和賞／ ever　これまでの歴史の中で［強調用法］
l. 6   the blessings　恵み、素晴しいもの
l. 7   paradise　楽園、天国のような場所
l. 8   Swat　パキスタンの北、美しい山並みが広がる渓谷地帯
l. 9   henna　ヘンナ（ミソハギ科の熱帯植物で、赤い染料が取れる）
l. 10 patterns　文様
l. 11 mathematical formulas and equations　数学の公式と方程式
l. 12 had a thirst for ...　〜を強く望んでいた、渇望していた
l. 15 excel in ...　〜の分野で優れている、秀でている

But things did not remain the same. When I was in Swat, which was a place of tourism and beauty, suddenly changed into a place of terrorism. I was just ten that more than 400 schools were destroyed. Women were flogged. People were killed. And our beautiful dreams turned into nightmares. Education went from being a right to being a crime. Girls were stopped from going to school.

　When my world suddenly changed, my priorities changed too. I had two options. One was to remain silent and wait to be killed. And the second was to speak up and then be killed. I chose the second one. . . .We could not just stand by and see those injustices of the terrorists denying our rights, ruthlessly killing people and misusing the name of Islam. . . . The terrorists tried to stop us and attacked me and my friends who are here today, on our school bus in 2012, but neither their ideas nor their bullets could win ....

　.... Many children ... especially in India and Pakistan are deprived of their right to education because of social taboos, or they have been forced into child marriage or into child labor. One of my very good school friends, the same age as me, who had always been a bold and confident girl, dreamed of becoming a doctor. But her dream remained a dream. At the age of 12, she was forced to get married. And then soon she had a son, ... I know that she could have been a very good doctor. But she couldn't ... because she was a girl ....

(483 words)

Notes

l. 17　**a place of tourism**　観光地
l. 19　**were flogged**　鞭で打たれた
l. 21　**a right**　権利／**were stopped from ...**　～するのを禁止させられた
l. 22　**my priorities**　優先順位、まず先にやるべきこと
l. 25　**stand by and see**　傍観する／**injustices**　不当な行為／**ruthlessly**　無慈悲に
l. 29　**are deprived of ...**　～を奪われる
l. 30　**have been forced into ...**　～を強いられてきた／**child marriage**　幼少での結婚
l. 31　**child labor**　児童就労
l. 32　**bold and confident**　大胆で自信に満ちた
l. 34　**could have been ...**　～になれたであろうに［仮定法過去完了］

Graphic Organizer

Malala's Life Events

- Malala was born in **1.** _____.
- She and her friends loved **2.** _____.
- They had big **3.** _____.

⬇

- Terrorists **4.** _____ schools.
- People were **5.** _____.
- Girls were **6.** _____ from going to school.

⬇

- Malala chose to **7.** _____ up against the **8.** _____ of the terrorists.
- Terrorists **9.** _____ her but she survived.
- She **10.** _____ the Nobel Peace Prize.

Malala's Message

All **11.** _____ should be allowed to receive **12.** _____.

Active Learning

1. Opinion Exchange

身の回りにある女性と男性の格差や不平等について話し合ってみよう。比較級を使いながら以下の場面を例に、話し合ってみよう。

例) Women are much more discriminated against in sumo. They are not allowed to enter the sumo ring.

◆ Sports
◆ School uniform
◆ Pay
◆ Women-only passenger cars
◆ Housework
◆ Others

[Key Words]
gender inequality
gap
equal
reverse discrimination
compete
athlete
preferential treatment
bias toward

Tips 違いの程度が大きいとき、much, a lot, far を比較級の前で使って表現します。度合いが小さいときは、a bit, a little, slightly などを用います。

(例) Women are <u>much more</u> discriminated against in sumo. They are not allowed to enter the sumo ring.
The salaries of men in our company were <u>slightly lower</u> than those of women.

2. Scenario

あなたは、X さんの事故を目撃しました。Key Words の語をいくつか使い、その様子についてシナリオを考えてみよう。

"One morning, when I was _____
I saw ... _____
It's quite certain ... _____
He/She must have ... _____
I predict ... _____
I wouldn't be surprised if ... _____
I'm quite sure he/she did ... _____
_____
_____ There can't be any doubt about it."

[Key Words]
survive
destroy
force
remain
attack
ban
realize
deny
kill
change
deprive
injure
hit
shot by
misuse

Tips 確かなことや憶測を述べるとき、このような表現が使えます。

I'm quite sure he/she did.	He/She must have ...	It's quite certain ...
There can't be any doubt about it.	May be ...	It's possible ...
I wouldn't be surprised if ...	I predict ...	

Further Thinking

1. What problems does child marriage create?
2. Make a list of ten reasons why education is important.

Words in Action

「キーワード読み」

　　Unit 6 では、意味のまとまりごとに区切って読んでいく読み方を練習しました。その区切った単語のグループ内には、メッセージの伝達上中心となる語があるはずです。その語のことをキーワードと呼ぶことにしましょう。マララのスピーチの一部を使って、意味ごとに区切り、その中のキーワードを見てゆきましょう。

> . . . **Education** is one of the **blessings** of life//—and one of its **necessities**.// That has been my **experience**//during the **17 years** of my life.//In my paradise home, **Swat**,// I always loved learning//and discovering **new things**.//I **remember**//when my **friends** and I//would decorate our **hands**//with **henna** on special **occasions**.//And instead of drawing **flowers** and **patterns**//we would paint our **hands**//with mathematical **formulas** and **equations**.

　　太字で示した語がその区切りの中のキーワードです。その単語、特にその単語のアクセントの置かれた部分を強く声の音程を高めにして読んでみましょう。あなたの音読にメリハリが付き、分かりやすくなるはずです。

　　区切りを付けることやキーワードを考えることは、その英文が何を一番伝えたいのかを考えるよいきっかけになります。例えば、以下のような文があったとしましょう。

> The title of my speech is my wonderful experience in Japan.

　　これは自分のスピーチのタイトルの紹介する文ですので、is の後で区切るのがいいことが分かります。前半の部分のキーワードは、The **title** of my speech is とするのが一般的ですが、「自分の」と言うことを強調したければ、The title of **my** speech is となるでしょう。後半の my wonderful experience in Japan も、「自分の」ということを言いたいのか、「素晴しい」ということなのか、「経験」なのか、それとも「日本」ということなのかによって、キーワードが変わり、言いたいことが変わってきます。このようにキーワードを考えることは、英文のメッセージを理解するよい練習になります。友達同士でどの語をキーワードにすべきかを話し合ってみましょう。

Unit 11
Eating Disorders

iStock.com/katiko-dp

Let's Chat

1. What would you put on the plate to eat healthily?

2. Have you ever tried dieting? Do you want to go on a diet?

Eating Disorders

When we think of eating disorders, we sometimes think that they are the result of a choice, but, in actual fact, eating disorders are serious illnesses. Eating disorders come in many forms. There are three major forms of eating disorder: anorexia nervosa, bulimia nervosa, and binge eating. Let us look at these in detail.

In the case of anorexia nervosa, a person eats very little because he or she sees himself or herself as overweight, although that person may in fact be dangerously underweight. How can we recognise such a person? Firstly, a person suffering from anorexia nervosa looks extremely thin. Secondly, their main aim is to stay thin and not to have a normal weight. To this end, they will check their weight several times a day. Additionally, their self-image is influenced by ideas of body shape in the media and by others. The person's health can be affected in many ways. For example, he or she might have extreme constipation and a weakening of the bones. Anorexia nervosa is also a mental disorder that has a higher suicide rate in women than in most other mental disorders.

Notes

Title eating disorders 摂食障害
l. 14 **constipation** 便秘
l. 16 **mental disorder** 精神障害

With bulimia nervosa, a person eats a large amount of food quickly and in an uncontrolled way, followed by efforts to take the food out of the body. This is known as 'purging'. The person achieves this in various ways. For example, he or she might exercise excessively. Alternatively, he or she will vomit up the food that they have just eaten. Another way to compensate for the large amount of food they have eaten is to take laxatives or diuretics, which force them to go to the toilet more than usual. Some other effects of this behaviour may be a badly swollen throat and badly-decaying teeth. Bulimia nervosa is different in one very significant way from anorexia nervosa, in that the person maintains a normal weight.

　　Lastly, binge eating means that someone eats a great amount of food very quickly in an uncontrolled way. In this case, the binge-eater is often overweight or obese, because he or she does not balance their over-eating with another activity such as exercising or purging. Such a person might eat until they feel uncomfortable, they might eat fast, or they might even eat when they are not hungry. There are also psychological factors. The person might feel ashamed or embarrassed about the way he or she eats.

　　We must remember that eating disorders are principally mental illnesses which have many forms and a wide range of origins. They should be treated appropriately by expert medical practitioners.

(432 words)

Notes

l. 20　**excessively**　過度に／**Alternatively**　あるいは、別な選択肢として／**vomit up**　吐く、嘔吐する
l. 21　**compensate for**　埋め合せる
l. 22　**laxatives**　下剤／**diuretics**　利尿剤
l. 24　**swollen**　腫れる、ふくれた／**decaying teeth**　虫歯
l. 25　**significant**　重大な、重要な
l. 29　**obese**　肥満の
l. 32　**ashamed**　恥ずかしい
l. 34　**principally**　主として
l. 35　**be treated**　治療される
l. 36　**expert medical practitioners**　専門の開業医

Graphic Organizer

Eating Disorders

There are three major 1. _____ of eating disorder.

Disorder	Anorexia Nervosa	Bulimia Nervosa	Binge Eating
Eating style	Eats very little because he/she thinks he/she is 2. _____	Eats a large amount of food quickly and uncontrollably, followed by 6. _____	Eats a great amount of food quickly and uncontrollably
Body weight	Underweight	7. _____ weight	Overweight
Symptoms & Characteristics	▶ Checks weight several times a day ▶ Influenced by ideas of body shapes in the 3. _____ ▶ Might have extreme constipation and weakening of the 4. _____ ▶ Has high 5. _____ rate in women	▶ Tries to take the food out of the body by 1) exercising 2) vomiting 3) 8. _____ laxatives or diuretics ▶ Might have badly swollen 9. _____ and badly-decaying teeth	▶ Does not 10. _____ over-eating with exercise or purging ▶ Eats until feeling uncomfortable ▶ Eats fast or eats even when not 11. _____ ▶ Might feel ashamed or 12. _____ about the way of eating

64 English through Active Learning —Read to Think and Speak—

Active Learning

1. Opinion Exchange

あなたが外食や食事を購入するとき、どんなことに気をつけてメニューを選びますか？該当する項目について、具体例をあげて意見交換しよう。

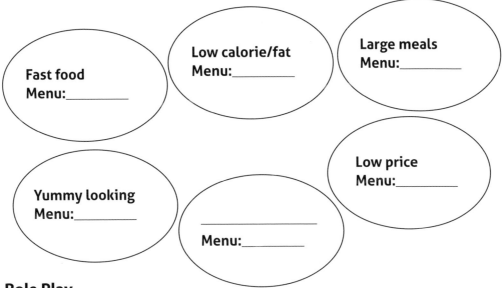

Fast food Menu:_____
Low calorie/fat Menu:_____
Large meals Menu:_____
Yummy looking Menu:_____
Low price Menu:_____
_____ Menu:_____

2. Role Play

栄養士役の人は、栄養表を参考に、話し手の食生活について、アドバイスをしてみよう。

Nutrient table

Function	Nutrient	Sources
Energy	Fats, Carbohydrates	bread, rice, potatoes, sugar, butter
Growth, Body building/repair	Vitamins, Minerals and Proteins	fruit, vegetables, milk, eggs, meat, fish, soybeans, yogurt, nuts, cheese
Digestion	Fibers	green leafy vegetables, water

Tips 人に何か行動を勧めるとき、このような表現が使えます。

I think you have to ...   I'm afraid you should ...   I don't think you can avoid ...

● Expressions for This Unit

What do you regularly have for breakfast/ lunch / dinner?   How often do you have ...?

eat out	eat at home	eat healthy	eat regularly	drink less coffee
sugar	salt	dairy products	junk food	nutrition
vitamin	soybean	cholesterol	alcohol	blood sugar level
hungry	uncontrolled	normal	natural	high calorie

Further Thinking

1. How does the media affect people's ideal image of the body? If you could decide the standard of how a human body should look, what would it be like?
2. Together with other groups members, create a healthy school menu with well-balanced nutrition.

Words in Action

「文頭の副詞と副詞句」

　　Unit 7 の「談話の流れ：文頭と文末の役割」の中で、その文がこれから言おうとしている事柄を予告する役割があることを取り上げました。Unit 11 ではさらにこの点について詳しく見てゆきます。

　　Unit 11 の本文では、主として順番を現わす副詞表現と、その文の話題を提示する副詞表現の2種類が使われています。順番を現わす副詞表現としては、Firstly、Secondly、To the end、Lastly、がありますが、これらの表現を見た読者は今から読む内容が、ある事柄の何番目の要素なのかというように、文章全体の中の個々の部分の位置づけを把握することができます。Additionally、For example、Alternatively などは、これから述べる内容が、これまでの内容とどういう関係にあるのかを示しています。一方、In the case of anorexia nervosa、With bulimia nervosa、In this case は、この後の文章のテーマを示しているいわば小見出しのような役割を果たしています。

　　これら以外にも、文頭には様々な副詞表現が用いられ、文章の流れをよくしたり、分かりやすくしています。話し手の気持ちを表す副詞表現としては、Surprisingly、Interestingly、Amazingly、Fortunately、Strangely などがあります。これらは、今から述べることは話し手にとって「驚くべき事だ」「興味深いことだ」などとその内容についての感想を予め示しています。

　　可能性について言及する副詞表現もよく使われます。Probably, Possibly, Maybe, Theoretically、In theory、Actually などは、この後に続く内容の可能性について話し手が予め言及しておくための表現です。同じように、態度を表明する副詞表現としては、Frankly、Honestly、Personally、In my opinion などがよく使われます。より観点や視点を絞った副詞表現としては、Academically、Economically、Politically、Financially、Technically などがよく使われます。コミュニケーションとは、本来予測しがたいものですが、それをできるだけわかりやすくし、これから伝えようとするメッセージの内容を少しでも理解してもらうために、このような副詞表現が使われています。

Unit 12　Working Conditions, Death from Overwork

istock.com / kieferpix

Let's Chat

1. What is the man doing? How do you think he feels?

2. What type of work environment do you prefer?

Working Conditions, Death from Overwork

'Would you like to die from overwork?' Most people asked this question by a future employer would probably answer 'No'. Nevertheless, this is the reality for many employees, especially in Japan. Many people think of Japan first partly because of the term 'karoshi', which means 'overwork death', but also because of social attitudes. Whether we accept that this is a true reflection of working conditions in Japan or not, we might find it useful to look at two particular areas, the causes of overwork and countermeasures that can be taken.

Common reasons that are given for overwork link this phenomenon to the attitude of the Japanese to work after the devastations of the Second World War. Japan was able to achieve an economic miracle by putting to use its national characteristic – a hard work ethic. In particular, Japanese workers are known for obeying their superiors with little complaint unless the demands put on them are obviously unfair. Additionally, they place a great deal of importance on maintaining a harmonious relationship with their colleagues. Moreover, by law, companies are allowed to ask their employees to work up to eighty hours overtime per month. However, the government only considers overwork to be a risk to a worker's health if the worker has worked over the maximum amount of legal working hours. It has been reported that overtime is not always recorded, and it is possible to understand that the amount of work some employees actually did might have led in some cases to their taking their own lives.

Notes

l. 5   social attitudes   社会の考え方／ **reflection**   反映
l. 10   devastations   荒廃、破壊
l. 12   national characteristic   国民の気質／ **a hard work ethic**   勤勉さ
l. 13   their superiors   彼らの上司
l. 15   a harmonious relationship   協調関係、「和」
l. 19   legal working hours   法定労働時間

The Japanese government has taken measures to protect workers in recent years after a number of high-profile cases of *karoshi* in the past decade were officially recognised. It has to be said, however, that such cases have existed since at least the 1980s, when the Japanese economic Bubble reached its highest point. Starting in 2014, a law was passed urging the government to heighten awareness of death and illness from overwork. The resulting 2016 study led to the formation of a government panel to look into ways of changing the workplace situation. Some of the measures taken in the past or recommended by the government have included encouraging workers to go home early on certain days of the week. It also promoted "telework", which means using mobile phones or computers in places which are closer to home. Despite these proposals, some companies have resisted these measures, or employees have felt pressure to continue working overtime without pay.

Perhaps the most effective way of dealing with the problem would be for the government to make a good life-work balance for everyone its main goal.

(439 words)

Notes

l. 23 **has taken measures**　対策を取ってきた
l. 24 **high-profile cases**　人目をひく、注目される事例
l. 26 **economic Bubble**　バブル経済
l. 29 **a government panel**　政府の委員会
l. 34 **resisted**　抵抗する

Graphic Organizer

Working Conditions in Japan

'**1.**_____' is the reality for many employees in Japan.

Causes of Overwork

1. Japanese hard work **2.**_____ (such as obeying their **3.**_____)

2. Maintaining **4.**_____ relationship with colleagues is valued

3. Companies can ask employees to work up to **5.**_____ hours overtime per month

Countermeasures

To protect the **6.**_____, the Japanese government
1) **7.**_____ workers to go home early on certain days of the week.
2) promoted "**8.**_____."

However,
▶ Some companies **9.**_____ these measures.
▶ Employees felt **10.**_____ to continue overtime work.

Therefore,
A good **11.**_____ balance for everyone should be the government's main **12.**_____.

Active Learning

1. Role Play
外国人役の人が日本の過労死の実情について聞いてみよう。説明をする人はテキストの内容を参考に、相手にわかりやすく教えてあげよう。

[外国人役]	[解説者]
What is *Karoshi* in Japan?	*Karoshi* means ...
What makes *Karoshi* so problematic?	*Karoshi* is caused by ...
What are the possible solutions for *karoshi*?	As a part of the solution, ...

2. Problem Solving
あなたが運営に関わる会社では、過労死の心配が指摘されています。1）どんな問題が生じていますか？ 2）どんな解決策、改善策がありますか？各自の会社について紹介し、グループで案を出し合い、意見をまとめて会社の取り組みを発表し合おう。

Company's Name _____

Work contents _____

Number of employees _____

Number of paid-leave days _____

Problems　　　Where?　　　Who?　　　What?　　　Why?

Actions _____

Solutions _____

Tips　不満や改善点について話し合うとき、このような表現が使えます。

I want to complain about ...	What can you do about ...?	Can you do anything about ...?
I'm sorry to say this, but ...	Something must be done ...	I'm not at all satisfied with ...
I must object to ...	Would you please not ...	Have you thought about –ing?

● Expressions for This Unit

government	employees	employer	home	companies
overwork	overtime	life-work	colleagues	amount
absent on leave	hourly-paid	legal	awareness	health
economic	unfair	obey the law	protect	resist

Further Thinking

1. The best life-work balance may depend on your daily priorities, such as achievements and enjoyment (e.g. pride, satisfaction, a sense of well-being, love, happiness, the joys of accomplishment). Think about how recently you have achieved and enjoyed something just for yourself.
2. Research the issue of burnout happening in the workplace today (e.g. school teachers, social workers, creators).

Words in Action

「相手を変えて同じ内容を繰り返し説明する」

読む力を話す力に変えてゆく方法について、Unit 12 を使って考えてみましょう。

- まずは本文を註釈や辞書などを使ってその内容を理解しましょう。
- 次のページの GO や AL の課題をやり、本文の内容を深く理解してみましょう。
- Unit 6 でやった区切り読みや Unit 10 でやったキーワード読みをやります。意味のまとまりごとに区切って読める、その中のキーワードがどれだか分かることが大切です。
- キーワードを書き出してみましょう。この段階まで来ると、キーワードを見ただけで本文の内容が頭に浮かんでくるはずです。
- Unit 12 の本文は全部で 439 語あります。1 分間に 120 語の割合で音読しても、およそ 4 分かかります。その本文をキーワードを見ながら、そのキーワードを含めて自分の英語で 2 分間にまとめてみましょう。本文をまねたり、本文を暗記したりする必要はありません。あくまでも、自分の英語でキーワードをつなぎ合わせ、意味内容を 2 分間でしっかりと英語で言えるようにしましょう。
- 2 列に並んで、向かい合って座ってみましょう。その人に、2 分間で本文の内容を伝えてみましょう。その時に、キーワードのリストを見てもかまいません。
- 次に、聞き役だった人が本文内容を 1 分 50 秒で話し役だった人に同じように伝えます。同じ内容なので、10 秒少なくとも同じように本文内容を伝えられるでしょう。
- ペアを変えて、1 分 40 秒で、同じように本文内容を英語で相手に伝えます。
- 次に、聞き役だった人は、相手方に 1 分 30 秒で同じように本文内容を伝えます。

この練習のポイントは、よく分かっている内容をキーワードを交えて自分の言葉で伝えること、そしてその時間を 10 秒ずつ短くしてゆくことです。3 ペア目の最後の人は 1 分 10 秒で伝えなければなりません。とにかくポイントを絞り、内容を端的にまとめて言う必要がありますので、注意は自然と言語形式から言語内容へと移ってゆきます。そのプロセスにおいて話す力が高まってくると考えられています。

Unit 13
Emotional Robots

istock.com / YakobchukOlena

Let's Chat

1. What do you think the man and robot are talking about?

2. Do you think robots need emotions? Why or why not?

Emotional Robots

Robots may one day become smarter than us, some science fiction writers declare, but they won't be able to cry.

Actually, that may not be true. Scientists are now understanding the true nature of emotions. First, emotions tell us what is good for us and what is harmful. The vast majority of things in the world are either harmful or not very useful. When we experience the emotions of "like," we are learning to identify the tiny fraction of things in the environment that are beneficial to us.

In other words, one of the chief purposes of emotions is to give us values, so we can decide what is important, what is expensive, what is pretty, and what is precious. Without emotions, everything has the same value, and we become paralyzed by endless decisions, all of which have the same weight. So scientists are now beginning to understand that emotions, far from being a luxury, are essential to intelligence.

In the future, scientists may be able to create rescue robots – robots that are sent into fires, earthquakes, explosions, etc. They will have to make thousands of value judgments about who and what to save and in what order.

Emotions are also essential if you view the evolution of the human brain. First, you have the reptilian brain, found near the base of the skull, which makes up most of the brain of reptiles. Primitive life functions, such as balance, aggression, territoriality, searching for food, etc., are controlled by this part of the brain.

Notes

l. 2　**declare**　断言する
l. 5　**harmful**　害を及ぼす
l. 7　**tiny fraction**　ほんの小さな部分／**beneficial**　利益をもたらす、有益である
l. 12　**a luxury**　贅沢品
l. 14　**rescue robots**　救助ロボット
l. 15　**explosions**　爆発
l. 16　**value judgments**　価値判断
l. 18　**reptilian brain**　爬虫類の脳／**the base of the skull**　頭蓋骨の基底部
l. 19　**Primitive life functions**　原始的な生きるための機能
l. 20　**aggression**　攻撃性／**territoriality**　縄張り制

At the next level, we find the monkey brain, or the limbic system, located in the center of our brain. Animals that live in groups have an especially well-developed limbic system.

Finally, we have the front and outer layer of the brain, the cerebral cortex, the layer hat defines humanity and governs rational thought. While other animals are dominated by instinct and generics, humans use the cerebral cortex to reason things out.

If this evolutionary progression is correct, it means that emotions will play a vital role in creating autonomous robots. So far, robots have been created that mimic only the reptilian brain. They can walk, search their surroundings, and pick up objects, but not much more. Social animals, on the other hand, are more intelligent than those with just a reptilian brain. Emotions are required to socialize the animal and for it to master the rules of the pack.

Sony experimented with these emotional robots when it manufactured the AIBO (artificial intelligence robot) dog. It was the first toy to realistically respond emotionally to its master, albeit in a primitive way.

In the future, robotic pets that form an emotional attachment to children may become common. Although these robot pets will have a large library of emotions and will form lasting attachments with children, they will not feel actual emotions.

(474 words)

Notes

l. 22　**the limbic system**　大脳辺縁系
l. 25　**the cerebral cortex**　大脳皮質
l. 26　**rational thought**　合理的思考
l. 27　**are dominated**　支配されている／**instinct**　本能／**generics**　遺伝的特徴
l. 30　**autonomous robots**　自立型ロボット
l. 31　**mimic**　まねる
l. 32　**Social animals**　社会的動物
l. 34　**pack**　群れ
l. 35　**experimented with ...**　〜を使って実験した／**manufactured**　製作した
l. 37　**albeit**　であるけれども
l. 38　**an emotional attachment**　感情としての愛情
l. 40　**lasting attachments**　永続的な愛情

Graphic Organizer

Robots with Emotions

1. _____ may be necessary to a robot's intelligence.

Reason 1

Emotions give us **2.** _____, so we can decide what is important, expensive, pretty, etc.

Some robots (e.g. **3.** _____ robots) will need emotions to make value **4.** _____.

Reason 2

Robots that mimic the **5.** _____ brain have been created, but the monkey brain will be necessary in creating **6.** _____ robots.

- **I. Reptilian brain**
  Robots that walk, **7.** _____ their surroundings, and pick up **8.** _____, etc.

- **II. Monkey brain**
  Robots that **9.** _____ emotionally (e.g. robotic **10.** _____ such as AIBO)

- **III. Cerebral cortex**
  Defines **11.** _____ and governs **12.** _____ thought

Active Learning

1. Opinion Exchange

Caring robots for the elderly (nursing robots) の開発が進んでいますが、ロボットの機能にどんな利点 (advantages) と欠点 (disadvantages) が考えられるか、お互いに意見交換してみよう。

A robot ...	Advantages	Disadvantages
that has a friendly humanoid face		
that can check health problems		
that can remind us of daily tasks		
that can retain phone numbers and names		
that can communicate enough to encourage the elderly		
that can heal the elderly by reading and responding to human emotions		

例）Realistically, I doubt that robots can become friendlier than humans, but I'm sure that they can entertain the elderly by playing cards and games.

Tips 確信していること、あるいは不確かなことを言うとき、このような表現が使えます。

I'm sure that ...　　I'm certain that ...　　I'm not convinced, but ...　　I doubt that ...

2. Scenario

AI ロボットが日常化した未来の生活を想像し、あなたの理想のロボットと過ごす生活をプランしよう。またその生活がもたらす恩恵と弊害についても考えてみよう。

Day

- 例）A robot would play my favorite music every morning to help me wake up.
-
-

Night

- 例）I don't want it to ..., because ...
-
-

Tips 願望やその逆を言いたいとき、このような表現が使えます。

I hope ...　　I was hoping that ...　　Hopefully ...　　I wish a robot could ...
I'm not too happy about ...　　I'm worried about ...

● Expressions for This Unit

harmful	expensive	valuable	beneficial	precious
autonomous	helpful	emotional	smart	order
primitive	intelligent	dominated	controlled	realistically
clean the house	take out the trash	diagnose my medical symptoms		suggest treatment
give me suggestions on what to wear		help me with my homework		cook meals

Further Thinking

1. Will the robots of the future be our good friends or enemies?
2. What do you think about utilizing humanoid robotics for language learning? What are the pros and cons?

Words in Action

「文脈からの意味の類推」

　私たちが英語を読んでいると、どうしても知らない単語や表現が出てきます。どうしても分からないキーワードは辞書を引く必要がありますが、本文中にその単語に意味を理解するヒントが隠されていることがよくあります。

　本文の第5、第6、第7パラグラフには脳に関する専門的な用語やなじみのない単語が出てきます。その一つが、reptilian brain でしょう。その1行下に reptiles という言葉が出てきますので、それと関係した brain であることは分かります。その直後に、Primitive life functions という表現があります。この primitive という語がヒントになります。「原始的な」という意味ですが、reptilian とは、「爬虫類に代表されるような原始的な」という意味で使われていますので、たとえ reptilian、reptile が分からなくとも、primitive が分かればその実質的な意味は理解できたことになります。さらに文章構成を見てゆくと、

　　第5パラグラフには、First ... reptilian brain ... Primitive life functions such as ...
　　第6パラグラフには、At the next level ... the monkey brain, or the limbic system
　　第7パラグラフには、Finally ... the cerebral cortex ... humanity ... rational thought ... humans use ...

と続いています。これを見ると、脳が発達していく過程で新しくできた脳の部位とその機能が示されていることが理解できます。たとえ reptilian brain、limbic system、cerebral cortex という専門用語が分からなくとも、本文内容はかなり理解できます。

　さらに例示や言い換えも、分からない用語や表現を理解するよいヒントになります。rescue robots の後には、– robots that are sent into fires, earthquakes, explosions, etc. と、Primitive life functions の後にも、such as balance, aggression, territoriality, searching for food, etc. と例示が、the monkey brain の後には、or the limbic system と or を使って言い換えた形で専門用語が示されています。このように、例示、言い換え、文章構成に注意を払うと、未知語を理解するヒントが随分と隠されていることがわかります。

Unit 14
Maslow's Hierarchy of Needs

iStock.com/Rawpixel

Let's Chat

1. What is the man drawing? What do you think they are discussing?

2. What are the top five things you cannot live without?

Maslow's Hierarchy of Needs

Maslow's 'Hierarchy of Needs' is a model used in economics and business to identify people's needs. Specifically, the model is a pyramid and it is divided into five sections. These sections cover the five main human needs. These are physiological, security, belonging, esteem, and personal accomplishment needs. Let us look at the various levels of the pyramid and see how they can be applied to the world of economics and business.

On the first level we have physiological needs; that is to say, everything relating to the physical or personal. At our most basic level we need air, food, and sleep. We also need shelter and warmth. On the second level, we have security needs. These are all the things that make us feel safe, such as having employment, financial security, and good health. On the third level, we have to consider the idea of belonging. By 'belonging', we mean belonging to different social groups, such as our family, but this can be extended to our friends and to different social groups of which we feel a part. On the fourth level, we think of esteem or recognition. Esteem refers to the way that other people see us in terms of social status. For example, do we have a good job and do we have good position in that job? How much money and how much power do we have? These are all aspects that go towards giving someone a sense of esteem. On the fifth and final level, we talk about personal accomplishment. By 'personal accomplishment', we mean achieving our personal goals in life to the

Notes
Title hierarchy 階層性、序列
l. 2　**Specifically** 具体的には
l. 4　**physiological** 生理的な／**esteem** 尊敬、尊重
l. 8　**physical** 身体の、肉体の
l. 15　**recognition** 評価、称賛

extent that we are fully satisfied with being the best person that we can be. We should note that we can only progress from each level to the one above when the need lower down has been satisfied.

As an example of how we can apply this model to business, let us examine how a food product can be marketed. Let us take the example of food. On the first level, food satisfies the physical need to sustain ourselves for life. On the second level, from the point of view of the food industry, we need to eat food that is safe for us, meaning that it follows the correct health and hygiene standards. On the third level, of belonging, the food industry attempts to encourage people to share an inherited culture through the packaging of food that emphasizes traditional, festive, and cross-generational identities. For example, in the case of preparing a Christmas dinner, a particular brand for Christmas pudding might show a family happily sitting around a table enjoying their Christmas dinner. On the fourth level, of esteem, we can talk about how food can reflect our values in life by choosing food which is clearly labelled to show where it comes from and how it was made. Examples of this kind of labelling are foods that identify them as 'fair trade' products or being 'organically farmed'. Finally, on the fifth level, we might feel personal accomplishment if we start a wine business which makes inexpensive but good wine made from organically-grown grapes because this satisfies our need to express ourselves, bring pleasure to other people, and find a purpose in our lives.

(539 words)

Notes

l. 25 **be marketed** 市場に出される、販売される
l. 26 **sustain** 維持する／**for life** 生涯、死ぬまで
l. 28 **hygiene standards** 衛生面の基準
l. 30 **inherited culture** 受け継いだ文化
l. 31 **festive** 祭礼の、お祭りの
l. 33 **Christmas pudding** イギリスのクリスマスで食べるプラムなどで作った伝統的なお菓子
l. 37 **fair trade** （それを作った労働者に正当な賃金が支払われているなど）公正な取引で売買された
l. 38 **organically farmed** 有機栽培で作られた

Graphic Organizer

Maslow's Model in Business

Maslow's 'Hierarchy of Needs' can be applied in **1.** _____ and business.

Maslow's Hierarchy of Needs

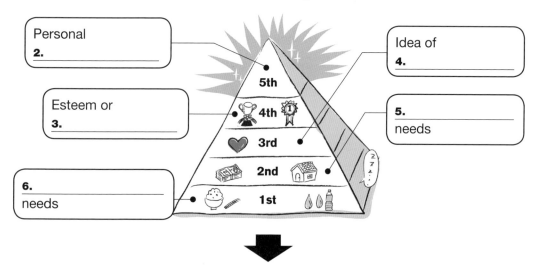

- Personal **2.** _____
- Esteem or **3.** _____
- **6.** _____ needs
- Idea of **4.** _____
- **5.** _____ needs

Application in Food Business

5th level	Start a business that satisfies our needs to **7.** _____ ourselves, bring pleasure to others, and find a **8.** _____ in life
4th level	**9.** _____ products to show where the food comes from and how it was made
3rd level	Encourage people to share an inherited **10.** _____ through the packaging of food
2nd level	Follow correct health and hygiene **11.** _____
1st level	Satisfy people's **12.** _____ needs to sustain their lives

Active Learning

1. Decision Making

Maslow の欲求段階説をもとに、Key words の具体例はあなたにとって、どのくらい重要ですか？相手と意見の相違がある場合、納得させて共通の優先順位を決めよう。

1st _____.

2nd _____.

3rd _____.

4th _____.

5th _____.

Others _____.

[Key Words]
travel   air
family   status
responsibility group
sleep   security
working group   fulfillment
law   stability
achievement   shelter
affection   personal growth

Tips 相手に納得してほしいとき、このような表現が使えます。
I really think it would be a pity if we didn't ...
It's a very good ... you know, better than ...!
Surely the most important thing would be to ...

2. Discussion

Maslow の欲求段階説を批判的に考えてみよう。21 世紀の自分たちに必要な欲求にはどんなものがあるか、根拠を述べながら紹介し議論しよう。

例) In my opinion, Wifi is the most important thing for us to live in the 21st century!
I agree with you. Also, we need to have technological skills and knowledge.

Tips 議論するとき、このような表現が使えます。
- I think the bottom level of the pyramid contains needs of ..., because ...
- The final level is the need to be ..., because ...
- I'm afraid I disagree with you. / I agree with you.
- What are your views ...?
- What about ...?
- Do you have any opinion on ...?

◉ Expressions for This Unit

generosity	a healthy life expectancy		freedom to make life choices
education	good government	health	income
social trust	social connections	shared purposes	salary
work-life balance	self-fulfillment	well-paid	

Maslow's *Hierarchy of Needs*

Further Thinking

1. Do you know someone who has achieved self-actualization? Describe the person and how they achieved it.
2. Let's find where the world's happiest countries are in the latest World Happiness Report. Compare the top three world's happiest countries with Japan, and discuss why Japan is not one of the happiest countries.

Words in Action

「メモからサマリーを書く」

　Unit 12 では、キーワードをメモ代わりにした話す力を伸ばす練習方法を紹介しました。この課では、Unit 14 の本文を使って同じような方法で、書く力を伸ばす方法を試してみましょう。

　やることは、話す力を伸ばす方法と途中までは同じです。註釈、G.O.、A.L. などを使ってしっかりと本文内容を理解しましょう。その後は、区切り読み、キーワード読みを行います。キーワードは書き出しておきます。さあ、キーワードを参考にしながら、本文内容のサマリーを書いてみましょう。

　この課の本文では5つの人間の欲求が順を追って説明されていました。各レベルにおける欲求とその典型的な例もありました。このように本文全体の内容やその論旨の展開もしっかりと理解して書き進めることが大切です。さらには、そもそもこの5つの段階とは人間の何を説明するためのものなのか、などといった基本的で根源的な事もしっかりと押さえておくと書きやすいです。キーワードの間を埋める英語表現は、本文で使われていたものでも、自分が既に知っている表現や、他の課で学習したものを使ってもいいでしょう。

　話す場合には身振り手振りなども使えますし、おおよその表現だけでも内容は通じますが、書く場合には、正確で厳密な表現の使用が求められ、その分ハードルが高くなります。書き上がったものは友達同士で交換をしてコメントし合ったり、間違いを直し合ったりするとよいでしょう。人の書いた英語を見るのは自分の英語の勉強になります。コメントなどを参考にして、もう一度書き直します。それをクラスの前でプレゼンテーションのように発表してみるとよいでしょう。自分が書くということを前提として本文を読むと、読み方も変わってきますし、単語の使い方や表現も自分が使うときのことを考えて、書き留めるようにもなります。今回はキーワードをメモ代わりに使いましたが、書くためのメモとして書き出してもかまいません。こういう練習を積み重ねることで、読む力が書く力に転化されてゆきます。

大学生のアクティブ・リーディング
―能動的思考・発信をめざす―

検印省略	©2019 年 1 月 31 日　第 1 版発行

編著者	鳥飼慎一郎
	鈴木夏代
	印田佐知子
発行者	原　雅久
発売所	株式会社 朝日出版社

101-0065　東京都千代田区西神田 3-3-5
電話（03）3239-0271
FAX（03）3239-0479
e-mail: text-e@asahipress.com
振替口座　00140-2-46008
組版・Office haru／製版・錦明印刷

乱丁、落丁本はお取り替えいたします
ISBN 978-4-255-15616-3 C1082

本書の一部あるいは全部を無断で複写複製（撮影・デジタル化を含む）及び転載することは、法律上で認められた場合を除き、禁じられています。